The Office Tr Book

By Christen Holly

Contents

QUESTIONS

SEASON ONE

1. What insect does Michael refer to when speaking to Jim in the opening scene?

2. What type of institution was Jim trying to sell to in the first scene?
    a. Library
    b. Law firm
    c. Grocery store
    d. Plumbing company

3. What is the special filing cabinet for things from cooperate?

4. What type of car does Dwight own in Season 1 Episode 1?
    a. '78 Toyota Corolla
    b. '78 280Z
    c. '78 Chevy C10
    d. '78 Plymouth Chrysler

5. How much did Dwight pay for his car in Season 1?
    a. $1,400
    b. $3,200
    c. $1,200
    d. $2,300

6. After fixing up his car, how much was Dwight's car worth?
    a. $3,100
    b. $2,000
    c. $3,000
    d. $3,200

7. According to Dwight, where is a hero born out of?
    a. A childhood trauma or out of a disaster
    b. From superhero parents
    c. Outer space
    d. Experiencing an alien abduction

8.   What name does Michael sign on his diversity acknowledgement?

9.   What healthcare plan includes acupuncture?

10.   What other service does the health plan cover?
      a.   Reiki Therapy
      b.   Therapeutic Message
      c.   Chakra Healing
      d.   Yoga

11.   True or False. Dwight considers healthcare in the wild to be like, "Ow, I hurt my leg, I can't run, a lion eats me and I'm dead".

12.   In Dwight's scenario of healthcare in the wild, what animal is he?

13.   How much is the deductible in the first healthcare plan that Dwight chooses for the employees?
      a. $350
      b. $1,300
      c. $1,200
      d. $550

14.   What is the name of the travel agency that Michael goes to, to plan a surprise vacation for his employees?
      a.   Scranton Travel Agency and Tour Guides
      b.   Scranton Tourism Agency
      c.   Scranton Travel Inc.
      d.   Scranton Travel and Activity Agency

15.   What is the address of the travel agency?
      a.   150 Adams Avenue, Scranton PA 18503
      b.   550 Turner Avenue, Scranton, PA 18503
      c.   1303 Adams Avenue, Scranton, PA 18503
      d.   150 Turner Avenue, Scranton, PA 18503

16.   At the travel agency, what is the first city that Michael suggests visiting with his employees?
      a.   Atlantic City
      b.   New York City
      c.   Los Angeles
      d.   Miami

17. While standing at Pam's desk, what two diseases does Jim write down as his medical conditions?
    a.   Ebola and Malaria
    b.   Ebola and Mad Cow Disease
    c.   Mad Cow Disease and Malaria
    d.   Bird Flu and Ebola

18. What disease causes your teeth to turn to liquid and then drop down the back of your throat?
    a.   Denta-Hydrosis
    b.   Spontaneous Denta-Hydrosis
    c.   Spontaneous Dento-Hydroplosion
    d.   Denta-Hydisia

19. How many feet does the mineshaft elevator drop?

20. How fast does the mineshaft elevator move?
    a.   Really Fast
    b.   Very Slowly
    c.   Normal Speed
    d.   Free-Fall

21. What is the actual name of the mineshaft elevator?
    a.   Company Coal Elevator
    b.   Rural Mineshaft
    c.   Industrial Coal Lift
    d.   Industrial Coal Elevator

22. What word is on the framed poster of skydivers on the wall behind Pam's desk?

23. What type of treat does Michael bring as a surprise for his employees after leaving Dwight to choose the healthcare plan?

24. What color is the Jell-o that Jim puts Dwight's stapler in?

25. True or False: Roy and Pam were originally supposed to get married in October but cancelled.

26. True or False: After cancelling their wedding the first time, Pam says they were planning on getting married sometime in the Spring.

27. What percentage did Michael increase profits in Season 1?
    a. 17%
    b. 27%
    c. 15%
    d. 21%

28. What did Michael cut so he would not have to fire a single employee?
    a. He cut office parties
    b. He cut the employees work hours
    c. He cut expenses
    d. He gave the employee more vacation days

29. Who asked Michael to be the Godfather of his child?
    a. A young Guatemalan guy who used to work in the office
    b. Dwight
    c. Todd Packer
    d. Dylan

30. What does Jim leave on Michael's desk before leaving the office at the end of the day?

31. What does H.E.R.O. stand for?

32. What diversity card does Pam receive to put on her forehead?

33. True or False: Oscar receives the Mexican diversity card to put on his forehead.

34. If Michael had a catchphrase for himself, what would it be?

35. Where does Dwight move the watercooler?

36. What term does Dwight use when asking if Stanley and Kevin have heard information going around the office?
    a. "What's the dealio?"
    b. "What's the gossip?"
    c. "What's up dogs?"
    d. "What's the scuttlebutt?"

37. Operation _____ _____ is the name of Michael's operation to plan a birthday party for an employee with the help of Pam.
    a. Operation "Morale Improvement"
    b. Operation "Morale Booster"

c. Operation "Birthday Booster"
d. Operation "Improvement Party"

38. What does Jim say when Dwight asks Jim if he wants to join an alliance with him?

39. True or False: Daryll is standing behind Dwight when Dwight crawls out of the cardboard box in the warehouse.

40. What color necklace is Phyllis wearing during Meredith's birthday party?
    a. Blue
    b. Pink
    c. Black
    d. Purple

41. What does Stanley write inside Meredith's birthday card?
    a. "Happy Birthday!"
    b. "Good News! It's Friday! Have drink and relax. Happy Birthday!"
    c. "Happy B-day. Sincerely, Stanley."
    d. "Meredith, good news: you're not actually a year older, because you work here where time stands still."

42. What does Pam write in Meredith's birthday card?
    a. "Happy Birthday!"
    b. "Best wishes. Happy Birthday, Meredith!"
    c. "Meredith, Happy Birthday. You're the best. Love, Pam."
    d. "Happy Birthday! Love, Pam."

43. When Michael hands Oscar a personal check, when does he tell Oscar to cash it?
    a. On Thursday
    b. On Friday
    c. On Tuesday
    d. On Saturday

44. Whose birthday is on the actual day of Meredith's birthday party?

45. What color is Jim's gym bag that he brought for their basketball game?
    a. Red
    b. Green
    c. Blue
    d. Silver

46.   What other item is Michael holding while carrying his gym bag in the first scene of the "Basketball" episode?
a.   His coffee mug
b.   A newspaper
c.   A notebook
d.   His jacket

47.   What time is the basketball game?
a.   Lunch time
b.   After work
c.   Before work
d.   While they are on the clock at work

48.   Michael says, "Blessed be those who ___ ___ ___".

49.   True or False: Phyllis and Kevin are alternatives for the basketball game.

50.   Michael compares basketball to what type of music?

51.   What does Michael say is a "classic beginner's mistake"?
a.   Not stretching before a game
b.   Eating before a game
c.   Not wearing the proper protective gear
d.   Being a ball hog

52.   The winner of the basketball game must buy dinner at what restaurant?
a.   Poor Richard's
b.   Chili's
c.   Farley's
d.   Alfredo's Pizza Café

53.   Michael calls a foul for what type of "aggression"?

54.   Michael tells Katy she is the new what?

55.   According to "Small Businessman", what is "one of the keys to success"?
a.   Decisiveness
b.   Loyalty
c.   Customer Service
d.   Money

56. What magazines is Michael subscribed to?
   a. American Way, USA Today, National Geographic
   b. Small Businessman, USA Today, American Way
   c. USA Today, Elle, Small Businessman
   d. Cosmopolitan, USA Today, Small Businessman

57. What place is like the "promise land" to Michael?

58. How did Dunder Mifflin move paper so fast in the 80's?
   a. The employees drank a lot of coffee
   b. The employees did cocaine
   c. The employees never took breaks
   d. The employees worked everyday

59. What are the names of the drink flavors inside Michael's car that Ryan finds while cleaning?
   a. Blue Blast and Artic Chill
   b. Crazy Cherry and Blue Blast
   c. Artic Chill and Lazy Lemon
   d. Blue Blast and Iceberg Chill

60. Where does Michael tell Ryan to put the drinks that he found in his car?

61. What does Dwight toss back and forth in his hands before deciding to ask Katy to go out on a date with him?
   a. A stress ball
   b. A pen
   c. A rubber band ball
   d. A tennis ball

62. What type of cologne does Ryan find in Michael's car?
   a. Drakkar Noir
   b. Rite Aid "Night Swept"
   c. Versace
   d. Cologne from Walmart

63. Michael's cologne is a "smell alike" to what cologne?
   a. Versace
   b. Drakkar Noir
   c. Christian Dior "Sauvage"
   d. Prada L'homme Prada

64. What type of food wrapper does Ryan find all over Michael's car?
    a. Gum wrappers
    b. Condom wrappers
    c. Hamburger wrappers
    d. Filet-o-fish wrappers

65. Roy and Pam are going to help Roy's cousin move because of what?

66. People tell Michael he has what type of face?
    a. Ugly Face
    b. An old face
    c. A very symmetrical face
    d. A handsome face

67. What is the make and model of Jim's car?

68. What is the color, make and model of Roy's truck?

69. Who is Michael's "someone special"?
    a. His employees
    b. His girlfriend
    c. His family
    d. His best friend

70. True or False: Michael says, he has an "everyday stand" every day with his employees.

71. Dwight wore what color shirt to play in the basketball game and what does it say?
    a. Brown, "World Gun Show"
    b. Dark blue, "Gun expo, Philadelphia 2002"
    c. Grey, "World Anime Show, Phoenix 2002"
    d. Black, "World Anime Expo, Philadelphia 2002"

72. True or False: Michael told Oscar to pick the new healthcare plan.

73. What does Roy say in front of Pam about Katy that makes her upset?

74. What type of women does Jim tell Roy that he likes?
    a. Blonde haired women
    b. Skinny women
    c. Moms
    d. Chubby women

75.   Who says, "You're a gentleman and a scholar" to a woman on the phone?

76.   In the very first episode of the series, what song is Dwight singing at his desk?

77.   Michael calls Jan, "Hilary Rodham _____".

78.   Why does Kelly slap Michael across the face?

79.   Why doesn't Dwight use the watercooler?

80.   What color does Angela think is kind of whore-ish?
      a.   Blue
      b.   Green
      c.   Pink
      d.   White

81.   What is Meredith allergic to?

82.   What type of cake does Michael want for Meredith's birthday party?

83.   Michael gives Meredith a birthday card that says what on the front?

84.   What type of charity is Oscar's nephew collecting money for?

85.   How much does Michael donate to Oscar's nephew's Cerebral Palsy charity?

SEASON TWO

1. Where does Jim keep his past Dundies and why does he keep them there?
    a. In his bedroom on a shelf because he doesn't want them at work
    b. Hidden, because he doesn't want to look at them and get cocky
    c. At work on his desk, because he thinks they are funny
    d. He threw them away, because he thought they were stupid

2. Where does Dwight keep his Dundies?
    a. At home in a display case above his bed
    b. At work on his desk
    c. In his living room
    d. In display case in his home office

3. While Pam is watching the recorded past Dundie awards, Oscar wins an award for what?
    a. The sexy award
    b. "Best Accountant" award
    c. "Show me the money" award
    d. "Smartest guy in the office" award

4. How often does Michael say the "05/05/05" party happen?

5. What type of parties does Jan say Michael already had for the year?
    a. The "05/05/05" party, a luau and the tsunami relief fundraiser
    b. The "05/05/05" party and the tsunami relief fundraiser
    c. The "05/05/05" party, tsunami relief fundraiser, his birthday party
    d. The "05/05/05" party, 5k run party, tsunami relief fundraiser

6. Why is there no open bar at the Dundies?
    a. Because it's against the company's policy
    b. Because of Jan
    c. Because Meredith is an alcoholic
    d. Because Toby said, "No".

7. Who is walking out of the breakroom when Dwight sneaks into the women's restroom?
    a. Ryan
    b. Phyllis
    c. Meredith
    d. Toby

8. Dwight says, "having a bathroom is a _____".

9. Who does Meredith sit next to at the Dundies?
    a. Ryan
    b. Creed
    c. Stanley
    d. Phyllis

10. Who does Kelly sit next to at the Dundies?
    a. Toby
    b. Creed
    c. Ryan
    d. Meredith

11. Ryan switches from sitting with Jim to sitting next to who?
    a. Kelly and Creed
    b. Meredith and Kelly
    c. Meredith and Creed
    d. Stanley and Toby

12. What type of alcohol does Stanley drink at the Dundy awards?
    a. Glass of Red Wine
    b. Margarita
    c. Beer
    d. Cranberry and Vodka

13. At the Dundies, Pam asks "Are you going to finish that" to who?

14. What Dundie award does Kevin win?

15. Who does Kevin bring as his guest to the Dundies?

16. What was the name of the Dunder Mifflin CEO who resigned?
    a. Kenny
    b. Phillip
    c. Randall
    d. Randy

17. Who does Jim say he is in an office relationship with?
    a. A blow-up doll
    b. Karen
    c. Pam
    d. Katy

18. What type of music does Roy suggest for the car ride with Pam and Pam's mom?
    a. Rock
    b. Country
    c. Jazz
    d. Classical and oldies

19. What type of scoreboard does Oscar keep on his desk?
    a. Fantasy football league scoreboard
    b. Paper football scoreboard
    c. Tic-tac-toe scoreboard
    d. Office basketball scoreboard

20. What is "Hateball"?
    a. Basketball
    b. Fantasy football league for the office
    c. Oscar and Kevin's paper football game
    d. Oscar and Kevin's office basketball league

21. Why is it called "Hateball"?
    a. Because Oscar hates it
    b. Because Kevin hates it
    c. Because Michael hates it
    d. Because Angela hates it

22. Who should teach Jim "Dunderball"?

23. What is the numerical address of Michael's condo?
    a. 122
    b. 123
    c. 126
    d. 128

24. What color is the exterior of Michael's condo?
    a. Blue and White
    b. Blue and Grey
    c. Brey and White
    d. Blue

25. Who is the head of the condo association where Michael lives?
    a. Bill
    b. Tony
    c. Anthony

d. Dwight

26. Where does Dwight sell beets to?
    a. Restaurants
    b. Local stores and restaurants
    c. Farms
    d. At the office

27. What does the scented candle that Jim found in the men's bathroom smell like?

28. What does the scented candle represent?
    a. The office Olympics
    b. The office employees
    c. The eternal burning of competition
    d. The ending of the office Olympics

29. What colored yogurt lids do the employees use for the office Olympics?

30. What is the first office Olympics game that the office employees play?

31. What kind of mortgage did Michael get?

32. True or False: Dwight saw Carpenter Ants in Michael's new kitchen.

33. What does "Flonkerton" mean in English?
    a. Box of Paper Snowshoe Racing
    b. Paper Box Racing
    c. The Office Olympics
    d. Office Shenanigans

34. Who competes in "Flonkerton"?
    a. Kevin and Phyllis
    b. Phyllis and Oscar
    c. Phyllis and Creed
    d. Kevin and Oscar

35. Who wins "Flonkerton"?

36. What medal color does Kevin get?

37. What time are the closing ceremonies for the office Olympics?
    a. 1:00 PM
    b. 12:00 PM

     c. 3:00 PM
     d. 5:00 PM

38. What color medal does Michael get?

39. Why does Michael receive a medal?

40. What color medal does Dwight get?
     a. Blue (Bronze)
     b. Silver
     c. Gold
     d. White

41. What color medal does Jim receive?

42. What does Dwight use to try to put the fire out?

43. What games do the employees play outside after the fire starts?

44. True or False: Angela chooses 2 books for the Desert Island game.

45. What book does Phyllis pick for Desert Island?

46. True or False: Dwight picks the books, Physicians' Desk Reference and Harry Potter and the Prisoner of Azkaban for Desert Island.

47. What would Dwight put in his hollowed-out book for Desert Island?
     a. Waterproof matches, iodine tablets, beet seeds, protein bars and NASA blanket inside of the book
     b. Iodine tablets, beet seeds, protein bars and NASA blanket inside of the book
     c. Waterproof matches, iodine tablets, protein bars and NASA blanket inside of the book
     d. Waterproof matches, beet seeds, protein bars and NASA blanket inside of the book

48. What DVDs would Meredith bring to Desert Island?
     a. Legends of the Fall, Legally Blonde, Bridges of Madison County and Ghost
     b. Legends of the Fall, My Big Fat Greek Wedding, Legally Blonde, Bridges of Madison County and Ghost
     c. Legends of the Fall, Legally Blonde and Ghost
     d. Legally Blonde and Ghost

49. What color is Ryan's car?

50. What 5 DVDs would Pam bring to Desert Island?

51. What is Dwight's all-time favorite movie?

52. What is the name of the company that Jim and Pam send Dwight's resume to?

53. What websites do Jim and Pam post Dwight's resume to?
   a. Monster.com and Craigslist
   b. Monster.com
   c. Monster.com, Google and Craigslist
   d. Craigslist and Indeed

54. What type of Karate does Dwight practice?
   a. Goju-Ryu Karate
   b. Aikido
   c. Judo
   d. Jiu Jitsu

55. What county does Christian work for?

56. What is the first thing Michael orders at Chili's?

57. Who finds Michael's screen play, "Threat Level Midnight"?

58. How much did Dwight pay for his Fitness Orb?

59. Who writes a suggestion for the suggestion box that says, "the company needs better outreach for employees fighting depression"?
   a. Tyler
   b. Michael
   c. Toby
   d. Tom

60. What is the name of the heating and air company in the same building as Dunder Mifflin?

61. What suite is Vance Refrigeration in?
   a. 200
   b. 210
   c. 201
   d. 108

62. Why is Michael scared of the new IT guy?

63. What type of surveillance does Michael conduct on the employees?

64. What animal statue does Jim have on his desk in his bedroom?
    a. Lion
    b. Turtle
    c. Tiger
    d. Penguin

65. What musical instrument does Jim have in his bedroom next to his bed?
    a. Keyboard
    b. Guitar
    c. Piano
    d. Drums

66. What is the name of the song that Jim and Michael sing to Karaoke at Jim's party?

67. Who was drafted by Angela into the party committee to plan the office Christmas party?
    a. Ryan
    b. Oscar
    c. Pam
    d. Phyllis

68. What does Oscar receive as his secret Santa gift from Kelly?
    a. An oven mitt
    b. A notebook
    c. A shower radio
    d. Cologne

69. What is the name of the lake that the booze cruise is on?

70. What branch of the military was Captain Jack in?

71. True or False: Pam was a cheerleader in high school.

72. What is the name of the boat the employees were on for the booze cruise?

73. What date is Roy and Pam's wedding scheduled for?

74. What type of butter does Michael ask Pam to rub on his burned foot?

75. What is the name of Dunder Mifflin's building manager?
    a. Billy Miller
    b. Dylan Merchant
    c. Billy Merchant
    d. Nick Merchant

76. What did Ryan crush up into Michael's pudding?
    a. One extra strength Aspirin
    b. Two extra strength Aspirin
    c. Three extra strength Aspirin
    d. Four extra strength Aspirin

77. What is Dwight's middle name?

78. What restaurant does Michael take Jim to so he could cheer him up?

79. What is "Ram"?

80. Where is Michael's meeting on Valentine's Day?
    a. New York
    b. Scranton
    c. Ohio
    d. Canada

81. What day did Ryan and Kelly finally hook up?

82. What prize did Jim win for ninth place as salesman?
    a. Pizza from Alfredo's Pizza Kitchen
    b. Pizza from Alfredo's Pizza Café
    c. Pizza from Cojino's Pizza
    d. Pizza from Cojino's Pizza Café

83. What temperature does Oscar like the office to be?
    a. Around 67 Degrees
    b. Around 66 Degrees
    c. Around 68 Degrees
    d. Around 64 Degrees

84. What country does Jim tell Pam he is going to visit a few days before her wedding?

85. What day does Jim plan on leaving for his trip?
    a. June 7th

    b. June 8th

    c. June 10th

    d. June 5th

86. Who brings their kids to "Bring you daughter to work day"?
    a. Stanley, Meredith, Kevin and Toby
    b. Meredith, Kevin and Toby
    c. Stanley, Meredith and Toby
    d. Stanley and Toby

87. What is Toby's daughter's name?

88. What is Meredith's son's name?

89. What is the name of the show that Michael was on when he was a kid?

90. What is the name of the guy who recruiter Michael to sell calling cards?
    a. Jamie
    b. Jason
    c. Phil
    d. Chris

91. What does Oscar hate that Angela has in her cubical?

92. What superpower does Jim tell Dwight he has when he claims to move the coat rack?

93. What charity does Creed plan to give his winnings to for casino night?

94. What charity does Michael pick as his charity for casino night?

95. Where did the Dunder Mifflin's property manager meet his girlfriend?
    a. At work
    b. At Chili's
    c. At a bank
    d. In Physical Therapy

96. What city did Kevin claim to have won the world series poker tournament?

97. Who beats Kevin at Poker?

98. What is the name of the band that Roy hires to play at his wedding?

99. When does Jim tell Pam he loves her for the first time?

100.   Who does Pam call after Jim tells her he loves her?

SEASON THREE

1.   What is Jan's favorite clothing store?

2.   What color is Ryan's kurta that Kelly gives him for the Diwali festival?
     a.   Silver
     b.   Gray
     c.   Turquoise
     d.   Black

3.   In Season 3, Episode 6, what was Michael referring to when he asked Kelly "Why didn't you buy me one?"
     a.   A kurta
     b.   A breakfast sandwich
     c.   A coffee
     d.   A T-shirt

4.   What does Angela think Indian people eat at Diwali?

5.   Who does Michael take as his date to the Diwali festival?

6.   Why doesn't Pam want to go to the Diwali festival?
     a.   Because Roy will be there
     b.   She doesn't have a date
     c.   She doesn't like Indian food
     d.   She doesn't feel well

7.   True or False: Stanley celebrates Kwanza

8.   When Michael gives his PowerPoint presentation about famous Indians before the Diwali festival, what does he sneak pictures of into the presentation?

9.   When Michael passes out pamphlets of the Kamasutra to everyone in the conference room, what sexual position does Creed identify out loud to everyone?
     a.   The Union of the Monkey
     b.   The Union of the Flower
     c.   Flower Union

d.   Union of the Monkeys

10.   What does Carol dress up like at the Diwali festival?

11.   What is the name of the doctor at the Diwali festival that Kelly's parents want to set her up with?
    a.   Vijay
    b.   Bodhi
    c.   Wali
    d.   Abhay

12.   What song is playing when Roy walks into the Diwali festival and sees Pam dancing with another guy?
    a.   Beyonce- "Crazy in Love"
    b.   Jewel- "You were meant for me"
    c.   Jewel- "Hands"
    d.   Beyonce-"Halo"

13.   How long have Kelly's parents been married?

14.   What is Carol's last name?

15.   What job did Ryan first get after Dunder Mifflin hired him on full-time?
    a.   Regional Director
    b.   Regional Manager
    c.   Jim's old job (Junior Sales Associate or Salesman)
    d.   CEO

16.   What color is Prison Mike's bandana?

17.   Who does Prison Mike call a "biotch"?

18.   Who tells Michael that Oscar is a homosexual?
    a.   Oscar
    b.   Toby
    c.   Dwight
    d.   Jim

19.   What device does Jim tell Dwight to use to determine if a person is gay?

20.   According to Jim, what store sells the gay testing device?

21.   Dwight tries to look for the gay testing device at what store online after finding it was sold out elsewhere?

a. Brookings
b. Benchbrook
c. Brookstone
d. Brookbench

22. When is Michael leaving on his Sandals Jamaica trip?
    a. The day after tomorrow
    b. In three days
    c. Tomorrow
    d. In a few hours

23. What brand of computer does Jim have on his desk in Stamford?
    a. Dell
    b. HP
    c. It doesn't have a brand
    d. Acer

24. What crime was Roy charged with after Pam broke off the wedding?

25. Pam and Roy did what with their wedding food after Pam called off the wedding?
    a. They froze it
    b. They threw it away
    c. They never ordered food
    d. They gave it to the office employees

26. How many toasters does Stanley's house have now that Pam and Roy's wedding has been called off?

27. When Jim sent Dwight a package containing the gay testing device, Jim left a note inside the package. What did the note say?
    a. "Here you go!"
    b. "Gay detector!"
    c. "Hope this helps."
    d. "I hope you find what you've looking for."

28. What did Jan offer Oscar after he signed something saying he wouldn't sue after Michael kissed him?
    a. A three-month paid vacation and a company car.
    b. A three-month paid vacation
    c. A one-month paid vacation
    d. A two-month paid vacation and a company car

29. Oscar and Gil are going where for Oscar's paid vacation?
    a. The Bahamas
    b. Australia
    c. Europe
    d. China

30. What type of baby does Michael want to adopt after finding out Angelina Jolie adopted a baby?

31. According to Pam, a child adoption application could cost how much?

32. Creed tells Meredith that "Andrea" is the office bitch. Who was Creed really referring to?

33. What is the name of the business convention in Philadelphia that Dwight and Michael attended?
    a. Northeastern Mid-Market Office Supply Convention
    b. Northwestern Mid-Market Office Supply Convention
    c. Northeastern Market Office Supply Convention
    d. Northwestern Mid-Market Office Convention

34. What type of transportation do Dwight and Michael take to the business convention in Philadelphia?
    a. A car
    b. A limo
    c. A Taxi
    d. A train

35. What does Michael say that firemen should never leave behind?
    a. Their brothers
    b. Their axes
    c. Their equipment
    d. Fires

36. True or False: Michael thinks the reason why Jim transferred to Stamford was because he didn't like him as a boss.

37. How many packs of condoms does Michael bring to the business convention in Season 3?
    a. 4
    b. 7
    c. 2

d.   3

38.   What color are Michael's "fun jeans" that he brings to the business convention in Season 3?
a.   Blue
b.   White
c.   Green
d.   Black

39.   Michael refers to Josh, the regional manager at the Stamford branch, as the "poor man's ___ ___"?
a.   Best manager
b.   Best employee
c.   Michael Scott
d.   Dwight Schrute

40.   What was the hotel room number of Michael's room when he was at the business convention in Philadelphia during Season 3?
a.   310
b.   309
c.   308
d.   312

41.   What is Dwight's hotel room number at the business convention in Philadelphia?
a.   556
b.   558
c.   557
d.   550

42.   After being underestimated by Jan, Michael makes a deal with what company and then says, "Yeah, well, maybe next time you will estimate me."
a.   Cummberlin Mills
b.   Hammermill Products
c.   Cummberlin Paper Products
d.   Hammermill Industries

43.   What is the name of Kelly's friend who is the cartoonist for the local paper?
a.   Allen
b.   Mike
c.   Curtis
d.   Milo

44.   How does Pam's date come up with his cartoons?
      a.   He thinks about stuff that he sees, or he dreams them.
      b.   He just does it
      c.   He doesn't know
      d.   He doesn't work for the local paper

45.   What is Michael's cure for the Monday blues?

46.   What exit does Dwight tell Jan to pull over on where there is an outlet for
      Jan's favorite clothing store?
      a.   Exit 20
      b.   Exit 60
      c.   Exit 40
      d.   Exit 10

47.   What does Pam suggest for her old vacuum cleaner if Dwight doesn't work
      out as manager?

48.   What group does Dwight tell Angela she can oversee when Michael makes
      Dwight believe he has become manager?
      a.   The Accountants
      b.   The women
      c.   Everyone in the Party Planning Committee
      d.   All the employees

49.   What type of lease is does Michael's Sebring have?
      a.   A personal lease
      b.   A 6-month lease
      c.   A year lease
      d.   A corporate lease

50.   What type of company car does Dwight tell Michael that he is thinking
      about getting?
      a.   Something German with decent gas mileage
      b.   Something German
      c.   An electric car
      d.   A 1978 Corvette

51.   When calling to find Herr's Chips for Karen, Jim tells a supplier that he is
      who from what market and what store number does Jim give to the supplier
      over the phone?
      a.   Mike from the West Side Market, 6
      b.   Ken from the East Side Market, 6

c.   Mike from the East Side Market, 6

d.   Mark from the West Side Market, 4

52.   What was Dwight's grandfather re-buried in?

53.   How did the bird in Season 3 die?

54.   Who does Dwight tell to clean up after the bird's funeral?
   a.   The office employees
   b.   The warehouse workers
   c.   No one, he cleans it up himself
   d.   No one cleans it up

55.   Stanley wakes up every morning in a bed that is what?

56.   Why does Pam watch the movie "28 Days Later"?

57.   Why did Pam get the blockbuster movies mixed up?
   a.   She didn't look at the picture on the front of the video tape box
   b.   There are no pictures on the video tape boxes
   c.   She meant to mix them up to make Jim laugh
   d.   She didn't mix them up

58.   According to Stanley, how many days are left until the next "Pretzel Day"?

59.   What is the name of Michael and Dwight's rap song about Scranton?

60.   What is the suite number for "the office" in the building?

61.   What year is Dwight's car?
   a.   1980
   b.   1988
   c.   1987
   d.   1990

62.   Andy tells Dwight he should be an English professor at what university?

63.   What crime did Prison Mike never get caught for?
   a.   Stealing
   b.   Kidnapping
   c.   Stealing, robbing, kidnapping the president's son and holding him for ransom
   d.   Stealing and robbing

64.   According to Prison Mike, Ryan would be what in prison?

65.   What color marker does Michael use when he draws on the arm of his date at the Christmas party?

66.   What is the name of the waitress that served them at the Benihana restaurant?

67.   True or False: Kelly sings Pat Benatar's song, "We Belong", to Ryan at the Christmas party

68.   True or False: Creed sings a song by The Beatles at the Christmas party

69.   Who did Michael intend to send the picture of Jan to instead of the packaging department?

70.   What is the name of Jan's psychiatrist?
        a.   Dr. Perry
        b.   Dr. Terry
        c.   Dr. Berry
        d.   Dr. Garry

71.   What is the name of Michael's talking computer?

72.   Who is "long tim"?

73.   True or False: Michael used to go fishing at Lake Wallenpaupack with his stepdad as a child.

74.   How much did the shark weigh that Andy claimed to have caught off Montauk in the Hamptons?
        a.   100 pounds
        b.   80 pounds
        c.   120 pounds
        d.   70 pounds

75.   During Dwight's job search, how many resumes and trivia packets does he give to employers?
        a.   3 resume packets, 3 trivia packet-Professional Resume, Athletic and Special Skills Resume and Dwight Schrute Trivia
        b.   2 resume packets, 1 trivia packet-Professional Resume, Athletic and Special Skills Resume and Dwight Schrute Trivia
        c.   4 resume packets, 1 trivia packet-Professional Resume, Athletic and Special Skills Resume and Dwight Schrute Trivia

      d.   3 resume packets, 1 trivia packet-Professional Resume, Athletic and Special Skills Resume and Dwight Schrute Trivia

76.   Who would arrange Michael's toys on his desk in a pleasing way?

77.   Andy states, "Sorry I annoyed you with my friendship" to who?

78.   What does Kevin refer to Oscar's paid vacation as?

79.   True or False: After Michael was scraping gunk off his wall sockets with a metal spoon, he gave himself a nasty shock, which caused his "epiphery".

80.   What does Michael want his son to know after having his "epiphery"?

81.   Who helps Michael make his video to his future son?

82.   What is the name of the guy who plays Ben Franklin?
      a.   Phil
      b.   Kyle
      c.   Gordon
      d.   Mike

83.   What is the name of the stripper at Bob Vance's bachelor party?
      a.   Elizabeth
      b.   Katy
      c.   Cindy
      d.   Michelle

84.   What does the stripper eat off Pam's desk?
      a.   Beef Jerky
      b.   Life Savers
      c.   Skittles
      d.   M&M's

85.   While training Dwight to salivate at the sound of his computer chime, what mint does Jim offer Dwight?

86.   Why was Michael so mad during Phyllis' wedding ceremony?

87.   What color is the flag attached to the back of Phyllis' dad's wheelchair?
      a.   White
      b.   Yellow
      c.   Red
      d.   Green

88.   Michael says Phyllis and Bob Vance's celebrity name would be what?

89.   What was Phyllis' nickname in high school?

90.   Who goes missing at Phyllis' wedding?
        a.   Uncle Bob
        b.   Uncle Al
        c.   Uncle Bill
        d.   Uncle Allen

91.   Which 4 brands of candy bars does Michael throw into the crowd during
        his speech at Ryan's school?
        a.   Whatchamacallit, Reece's, Pieces, 100 Grand, Skittles
        b.   Whatchamacallit, Skittles, 100 Grand, Snickers
        c.   Whatchamacallit, PayDay, 100 Grand, Snickers
        d.   Whatchamacallit, PayDay, 100 Grand, Skittles

92.   What was the subject of the textbook Michael tore up in Ryan's class?
        a.   Business
        b.   Economics
        c.   Sales
        d.   Customer Service

93.   What type of art does Gil call Pam's art?

94.   What was in Michael's pocket when he hugged Pam at her art show?

95.   What type of food does Michael bring to David Wallace's party?

96.   Why does Michael think people might get sick from the food he brought to
        David Wallace's party?

97.   What does Pam tell Roy that makes him freak out at the bar?

98.   Why does Karen call Jim an agoraphobic?
        a.   He hates being around people
        b.   He hates going to restaurants
        c.   He would rather sit at home than go out to the movies with her
        d.   He never wants to go out with her

99.   What does Dwight do to Roy when Roy tries to attack Jim?

100. How many years has Dwight brought pepper spray into the office to protect himself and his fellow employees?
   a.   10 years
   b.   3 years
   c.   13 years
   d.   8 years

101. What type of house is Phyllis looking into buy near the river?
   a.   Waterfront property
   b.   A historical house
   c.   She isn't looking into buying a house
   d.   She already owns a house

102. How long does Dwight say he is going to shun Andy?

103. Why was Dwight shunned when he was 4 to 6 years old?
   a.   For not saving the excess oil from a Tuna can
   b.   For talking back to his parent
   c.   For not cleaning his room
   d.   For not saving beet juice

104. To get Michael off the roof, Pam tells Michael she has a present for him. What does Dwight tell Michael the present is?
   a.   A Repliee B1 Expo female robot
   b.   A Repliee T1 Expo female robot
   c.   A Repliee Q1 Expo female robot
   d.   A Repliee S1 Expo female robot

105. Who tells Michael he has a "Nerfy Life"?
   a.   Toby
   b.   Carl
   c.   Darryl
   d.   Oscar

106. When Jim impersonates Dwight, what type of device does Jim have attached to his belt?
   a.   Flashlight
   b.   Pager
   c.   Cell phone
   d.   Watch

107. How much did it cost for Jim to create his outfit to impersonate Dwight?
   a. $12.00
   b. $7.00

c. $11.00

d. $14.00

108.   True or False: The obscene watermark was on 24-pound Cream Letter Stock.

109.   When does Michael say, "They are trying to make me an escape goat"?

110.   What Does Dwight give Jim for his tardiness?

111.   What does Jim give Dwight if he does not complete a full report?
    a.   A Demerit
    b.   A" Dissajulation"
    c.   Nothing
    d.   He doesn't care if he completes his report

112.   True or False: Kevin was reading "Elle Magazine" while relaxing in the women's restroom at the office.

113.   What store does Angela like to shop in for colonial clothing?

114.   What is the first challenge Michael gives the employees when they are at the beach?

115.   What job does Michael give Pam while the employees are engaging in the challenges at the beach?

116.   Who cooks the hot dogs for the hot dog eating contest?
    a.   Michael
    b.   Pam
    c.   Dwight
    d.   Phyllis

117.   What characters actually do the coal walk?

118.   Creed is referring to what when he says, "swing low, sweet chariots."

119.   Who is Jim's opponent in the Sumo challenge?
    a.   Andy
    b.   Oscar
    c.   Stanley
    d.   Karen

120. What does Michael call the man with the white beard who works at corporate?

121. Why does Karen tell Jim not to feel bad for Jan?

122. What does Pam tell Karen before Karen interviews for the corporate job?

123. What did the note inside Jim's interview paperwork from Pam say?

124. What does Karen call Pam after Pam reveals her true feeling to the office employees when they are all at the beach?

125. Who does Michael imitate when he gets back to the office after not getting the corporate job?
    a.   Borat
    b.   The Terminator
    c.   The Joker
    d.   Batman

SEASON FOUR

1. What type of milk does Michael use while eating his cereal in the first episode of Season 4?

2. What type of video does Pam click on that gives her computer a virus?

3. What is the name of Angela's cat that Dwight mercy killed?
    a. Twinkles
    b. Sprinkles
    c. Princess Lady
    d. Mittens

4. What does Michael bring to the hospital as a gift for Meredith?
    a. Balloons
    b. A card
    c. A teddy bear
    d. Flowers

5. What question does Creed ask Meredith when they visited Meredith in the hospital?

6. What is the name of Michael's fun run for Meredith?
    a. Michael Scott DWSMPPDMC Rabies Awareness Pro-Am Fun Run Race
    b. Michael Scott DWSMPMC Rabies Awareness Pro-Am Fun Run Race
    c. Michael Scott DWSMPMC Rabies Pro-Am Fun Run Race
    d. The Scranton DSMPMC Rabies Awareness Pro-Am Fun Run Race

7. What type of problem does Andy have with nipples when he runs?

8. Who accepts the check made out to Science?
    a. Pam
    b. Meredith
    c. Elizabeth, the stripper
    d. Cindy, the waitress

9. How much is the check to science?
    a. $340

b. $500
c. $430
d. $543

10.   What does Michael eat right before the fun run?

11.   What does Pam buy from the estate sale?
    a.   A chair
    b.   A blanket
    c.   A shirt
    d.   A lamp

12.   What type of phone does Ryan give the employees?

13.   Who stole all of Michael's jeans when he was a kid?
    a.   His cousin
    b.   The foreign exchange student who lived with him and his family
    c.   His mother
    d.   A family friend who lived with them for the summer

14.   What is Mr. Dunder's first name?
    a.   Peter
    b.   Robert
    c.   Kyle
    d.   Mitch

15.   Who sign's Meredith's pelvis cast?

16.   The "Launch Party" sign accidently says what?

17.   What is the name of the bad pizza place?

18.   What is the name of the good pizza place?

19.   How does Dwight know the pizza delivery kid?
    a.   Through a family friend
    b.   He works for Dwight
    c.   He is the kid that steals hemp from his hemp farm
    d.   He sells beets to him

20.   How much was the pizza Michael ordered, not including tip or the coupon?
    a. $63.50
    b. $64.50
    c. $65.00

d.	$63.00

21.	How my much was Michael supposed to get discounted off the pizza with the coupon?

22.	How many pizzas did Michael order?
	a.	7
	b.	8
	c.	9
	d.	6

23.	What was the ice sculpture in the shape of?

24.	True or False: Andy bought the ice sculpture from a friend.

25.	Who stands in front of the door while the pizza delivery kid uses the restroom?
	a.	Dwight
	b.	Andy
	c.	Dwight and Andy
	d.	Michael and Dwight

26.	Who ends up paying for the pizza that was delivered by the pizza delivery kid?
	a.	Michael
	b.	Dwight
	c.	Andy
	d.	Jim

27.	What is the name of Andy's college singing group?

28.	What movie did Michael rent that made him treat Pam poorly?
	a.	The Devil Wears Prada
	b.	Slumdog Millionaire
	c.	Legally Blonde
	d.	Bridges of Madison County

29.	What does Michael do at night do earn more money?

30.	What does Dwight say, "is the lifeblood of the agritourism industry."?
	a.	Google
	b.	Yelp
	c.	Trip Advisor
	d.	Word of mouth

31. What type of furniture demonstration does Mose do for customers?

32. What reward does a Schrute man get when he has sex with another woman?

33. What is the name of Kevin's new band?

34. What is the name of Michael's boss at the telemarketing company?
    a. Nick Figaro
    b. Nick Filipe
    c. Robert Conelli
    d. Robert Giosi

35. What room themes are available at Schrute Farms?
    a. America and Nighttime
    b. Nighttime and Irrigation
    c. America, Farming and Nighttime
    d. America, Irrigation and Nighttime

36. Where does Michael run off to after he tells Jan he is broke?

37. What commercial song does Andy have trouble remembering the words to?

38. What computer game does Dwight play where he creates himself as a character?
    a. Second Life
    b. First Life
    c. Third Life
    d. My Second Lifetime

39. Dwight made his character in the computer game exactly the same as himself except for what?

40. Who helps create and sing the "Dunder Mifflin song"?
    a. Creed, Darryl, Andy, Kelly and Kevin
    b. Darryl, Andy and Kelly
    c. Creed, Darryl, Toby, Kelly and Kevin
    d. Darryl, Andy, Kelly and Kevin

41. What celebrity does Phyllis try to get into the Scranton branch commercial for Dunder Mifflin?
    a. Sue Grafton
    b. Sue Griffin

c.   Susan Tyler
d.   Susan Mitchel

42.   What does Angela call Andy while they are making out?

43.   Where do the employees watch their commercial for the first time?

44.   Who does Karen try to "steal" from the Scranton branch?

45.   True or False: Michael sets up a dummy with snoring sounds at his desk to make it look like he is sleeping in his office.

46.   What does Michael want Pam to write on the "wanted ad"?

47.   Who started the finer things club?

48.   Whose name is on the warehouse uniform that Jim wears to Utica?
      a.   Daryll
      b.   Carl
      c.   Madge
      d.   Nate

49.   What type of can does Dwight pee into on the way to Utica?

50.   What do Jim, Dwight and Michael try to steal from Utica?

51.   Who wasn't invited to the woods for a "get to know you weekend" and was upset about not being invited?

52.   Who says, "No more smores, no more smores."?
      a.   Kevin
      b.   Toby
      c.   Pam
      d.   Ryan

53.   What type of pie does Creed want for his birthday?
      a.   Pecan
      b.   Apple
      c.   Cherry
      d.   Peach Pie

54.   What is Michael trying to eat when Dwight tackles Michael in the forest?

55. What is the name of the whale that Andy requests for his birthday cake?
   a. Fudgy the Whale
   b. Pudgy the Whale
   c. Nellie the Whale
   d. Snuggy the Whale

56. What does Michael scream in the forest regarding Jan?

57. What did Jim attempt to do about the employees' birthday parties that upset the employees?

58. What does Pam bring to Michael when he is in meetings to make him seem busy?

59. How much money would Jan get by winning her case against Dunder Mifflin?
   a. $1 million
   b. $4 million
   c. $2 million
   d. $5 million

60. What is the name of Jan's new young male assistant?

61. Why does Jan steal Michael's personal diary?

62. Who is "just as hot as Jan, but in a different way"?

63. What is Jan's cheap suggestion for dinner after she and Michael leave her deposition?
   a. Mexican food
   b. Chinese food
   c. Italian food
   d. Fast food

64. Who is invited to Michael and Jan's Dinner party?

65. Who cries because they were not invited to Michael's dinner party?

66. What does Pam give Jan when she and Jim show up at the dinner party?
   a. Wine
   b. Flowers
   c. Nothing
   d. Pam didn't go to the dinner party

67. What is the name of Jan's candle company?

68. Which door is broken inside Michael's condo?

69. Where does Michael sleep so Jan can have the bed to herself?

70. How much did Michael pay for his Plasma TV?
    a. $300
    b. $200
    c. $500
    d. $100

71. What music does Jan play for her guests at the dinner party?

72. What does Jim say happened to his apartment so he could try to leave the dinner party?
    a. His apartment burned down
    b. His apartment flooded
    c. His apartment was burglarized
    d. He never said anything happened to his apartment

73. How did the sliding glass door shatter?

74. How much money does Michael try to get from Andy and Jim to become co-owners of Jan's candle company?
    a. $20,000
    b. $10,000
    c. $15,000
    d. $13,000

75. Who is Dwight's date at the dinner party?

76. What does Michael's neon sign say?

77. What does Jan throw at Michael's Plasma TV?

78. What does Jim steal from Jan and Michael's condo?

79. Who does Michael fall in love with while searching for a chair?
    a. Carol
    b. The Chair Model Lady
    c. A clothing model
    d. Pam's mom

80. What page is the chair model lady on?
    a. Page 28
    b. Page 92
    c. Page 58
    d. Page 85

81. Who does Phyllis try to set Michael up with?

82. Who does Pam set Michael up with?

83. Who does Kevin set Michael up with?

84. What does Michael order from Wendy's over the phone?

85. What is the Chair Model's name?
    a. Deborah Miller
    b. Deborah Shoshlefski
    c. Deborah Turner
    d. Deborah Shomen

86. How did the chair model die?
    a. Suicide
    b. Car accident
    c. Falling
    d. Drug overdose

87. Who are the families of Scranton Business Park?
    a. Dunder Mifflin, Vance Refrigeration, DisasterKits Limited, W.B Jones Heating and Air and Cress Tool and Die.
    b. Dunder Mifflin, Vance Refrigeration, W.B Jones Heating and Air and Cress Tool and Die.
    c. Dunder Mifflin, Vance Refrigeration, Disasters Limited, W.B Jones Heating and Air and Cress Tool and Die.
    d. Dunder Mifflin, Vance Refrigeration and W.B Jones Heating and Air

88. What is the name of Pam's Landlady?
    a. Lidia
    b. Cathy
    c. The show never reveals her name
    d. Sarah

89.   Who touches Pam's knee?

90.   What is the name of Ryan's friend who resembles a hobbit?

91.   What is the name of the security guard at Dunder Mifflin?

92.   What statement Stanley yell at Michael that causes Michael to fake fire him?

93.   What type of print does Michael leave in the wet concrete?

94.   What does Darryl say gang members use when someone gets in your face?

95.   True or False: Andy sells his Nissan Xterra to Dwight.

96.   What high school did Pam attend?
       a.   Scranton High School
       b.   Fisher Bohara High School
       c.   Valley View High School
       d.   Scranton Valley High School

97.   Why did Andy have blisters all over his hands?
       a.   From cooking
       b.   From riding his bike
       c.   Practicing for a golf game
       d.   From being burned

98.   What does Jim buy for the Goodbye Toby party?

99.   Who replaces Toby when he moves to Puerto Rico?

100.   Who Does Kevin see at the grocery store when picking up more bbq sauce for Toby's Goodbye Party?

SEASON FIVE

1. What is the prize for the branch who loses the most weight?

2. When starting the weight loss challenge, how much do all the Scranton employees weigh, excluding Pam?
   a. 2,315 pounds
   b. 2,210 pounds
   c. 2,300 pounds
   d. 2,203 pounds

3. What school does Pam get accepted to?

4. Who faints from not eating enough during the weight loss challenge?

5. Who does Dwight drop off in the bad part of town to get them to walk all the way back to the office to burn calories for the weight loss challenge?

6. What is the name of Michael's "fat person" character?

7. What time does Jim tell Pam to meet him when he proposes to her?
   a. 2:00 PM
   b. 12:00 PM
   c. 1:00 PM
   d. 3:00 PM

8. What did Jim say exploded on him at the rest stop where he proposed to Pam?

9. How many pounds did Stanley lose during the branch weight loss challenge?
   a. 8 pounds
   b. 15 pounds
   c. 7 pounds
   d. 11 pounds

10. Meredith slept with someone in exchange for what?

11.   What is the name of the Scranton Rep for Hammermill that Meredith talks about in the ethics meeting?
        a.   Bruce Miller
        b.   Bruce Myers
        c.   Bruce Sampson
        d.   She never reveals his name

12.   What does Dwight use as a baby to help prepare Michael for the birth of Jan's baby?

13.   What does Dwight tell Michael to do with a sharpie immediately following the birth of Jan's baby?

14.   What brand of stroller does Jan bring to her baby shower?

15.   How much does Oscar say Jan's fancy stroller cost?
        a. $1,100
        b. $900
        c. $1,200
        d. $1,050

16.   How much does Dwight say he spent on his whole bomb shelter?
        a. $1,300
        b. $1,200
        c. $2,000
        d. $2,100

17.   Who does Jan tell Michael not to date?

18.   Where does Pam start working in New York because she ran out of money while in school?

19.   What do the thieves steal from Oscar's desk?
        a.   His wallet
        b.   His checkbook
        c.   The company's checks for payroll
        d.   His laptop

20.   What do the thieves steal from Kevin's desk?

21. What does C.R.I.M.E. -A.I.D stand for?
    a. Crime Reveals Innocence Makes Everyone Angry I Declare
    b. Crime Reveals Innocence Makes Everyone Aware I Declare
    c. Crime Reduces Innocence Makes Everyone Angry I Declare
    d. Crime Reduces Innocence No Money for Anyone I Declare

22. What does Kevin auction off at the C.R.I.M.E.-A.I.D. auction?

23. What type of gavel does Phyllis buy for Michael?

24. What does Jim bid on at the auction?

25. How much does Jim spend at the auction?
    a. $10
    b. $5
    c. $7
    d. $2

26. What does Phyllis dress up like for Halloween in Season 5?
    a. Raggedy Ann
    b. A lion
    c. An angel
    d. A judge

27. What does Meredith dress up like for Halloween in Season 5?
    a. A princess
    b. A cat
    c. A cheerleader
    d. She doesn't dress up

28. What is the name of Pam's friend at school who develops a crush on her?
    a. Allen
    b. Albert
    c. Alex
    d. Alec

29. How much did Kelly pay for her bridesmaid dress when Michael lied about being engaged to Holly?
    a. $50
    b. $100
    c. $200
    d. $150

30. Where does David Wallace send Michael abroad?

31. What computer programs does Pam say she hates because it made her fail art school?
   a. Flash, Acrobat and Quark
   b. Flash and Adobe
   c. Adobe and Quark
   d. Flash, Adobe and Quark

32. What is the name of the sushi restaurant that concierge Marie recommends to Andy?
   a. Sushi King
   b. Benihana's
   c. Matsuki
   d. Matsaki

33. What is Kelly brining to Toby when Michael find out Toby is back in the office?
   a. Files
   b. A brownie
   c. Cake
   d. A drink

34. What street is Jim's parent's house on?

35. Who lives by Jim's parent's house?
   a. Kevin
   b. Michael
   c. Creed
   d. Phyllis

36. Why does Ryan break up with Kelly in Season 5?

37. How much is the office's surplus?
   a. $4,400
   b. $4,100
   c. $4,300
   d. $4,000

38. How much will Michael get from the surplus if he keeps it for himself?
   a. $645
   b. $655
   c. $650
   d. $675

39. What was Michael initially going to buy for the office with the surplus?

40. What is the name of the German minister who Dwight uses to marry Angela without her knowing?
   a. Zeke
   b. Hansel
   c. Conrad
   d. Troy

41. How fast can Dwight skin a mule deer?
   a. In less than 5 minutes
   b. In less than 3 minutes
   c. In less than 10 minutes
   d. In less than 9 minutes

42. What is "Princess Unicorn's" catch phrase?

43. What is in the drink that Michael makes up called "One of Everything"?
   a. Equal parts scotch, rum, gin, vermouth, triple sec and one pack of Splenda.
   b. Equal parts scotch, absinthe, rum, gin, vermouth and three packs of Splenda.
   c. Equal parts scotch, absinthe, rum, gin, vermouth and two packs of Splenda.
   d. Equal parts scotch, absinthe, rum, gin, vermouth, triple sec and two packs of Splenda.

44. True or False: The name of the rehab center that Michaels brings Meredith to is Sunset Rehabilitation.

45. What are the five parts of the Schrute family five-fingered intervention?
   a. Awareness, edge, control, acceptance and punching
   b. Awareness, education, controlling, attacking and punching
   c. Awareness, education, control, acceptance and punching
   d. Awareness, edge, controlling, acceptance and punching

46. True or False: Toby pays Darryl $150 for his Princess Unicorn doll.

47. How fast does Michael think he was running when the traffic radar displayed his speed?
    a. 32 MPH
    b. 31 MPH
    c. 33 MPH
    d. 30 MPH

48. Whose desk did Angela and Dwight have sex on?

49. How many rules must all Schrute boys learn before the age of 5?
    a. 5
    b. 25
    c. 60
    d. 40

50. When did the owner of Prince paper open his business?

51. About how many clients does Prince paper have?
    a. 80
    b. 85
    c. 90
    d. 95

52. Name all the employees who do not find Hilary Swank hot?
    a. Kevin, Oscar, Meredith, Phyllis, Creed
    b. Kevin, Oscar, Phyllis, Toby
    c. Kevin, Oscar, Meredith, Phyllis, Toby
    d. Kevin, Oscar, Meredith, Creed

53. Who is the first person to notice the smoke from the fire that Dwight started in the office?

54. Who screams that they "need to grab their purse" while everyone is trying to get out of the building after Dwight sets the fire in the office?
    a. Pam
    b. Phyllis
    c. Meredith
    d. Kelly

55. What does Kevin destroy during the fire?

56. How much did the CPR dummy cost after Dwight destroyed it?
   a. $3,500
   b. $3,200
   c. $3,100
   d. $3,600

57. In sales, ABC means what?

58. What is the name of the CPR instructor?
   a. Kylie
   b. Michelle
   c. Rose
   d. Melissa

59. What type of girl scout cookies does Dwight buy from Toby?
   a. A case of thin mints
   b. A case of do-si-dos
   c. A case of chocolate chip cookies
   d. A case of peanut butter cookies

60. Who keeps refusing to sign Dwight's apology letter?

61. Who is the first to roast Michael at his roast?
   a. Angela
   b. Phyllis
   c. Pam
   d. Oscar

62. Who would Kelly make out with before she'd make out with Michael?
   a. Anybody from the warehouse
   b. A statue
   c. Phyllis
   d. Bob Vance

63. What caption did Michael write under the picture he posted on the bulletin board of Meredith's boobs?

64. What is the name of the character that Jack Black plays in the movie that Andy, Pam and Jim watch?
   a. Steve
   b. Mitch
   c. Sam
   d. Stan

65. What is the name of the Inn that Michael and Pam stay in when they are on the road for Michael's lecture circuit?
   a. The Lodge
   b. The Travel Inn
   c. Travel Right Inn
   d. Travel King Inn

66. Who forgot Kelly's birthday?
   a. Everyone
   b. Her parents
   c. Her sisters
   d. Her boyfriend

67. What kind of cake does Kelly want for her birthday?

68. What is the name of Angela's new cat?

69. How did Angela afford to pay for her new cat?

70. How much did Angela's new cat cost?
   a. $5,000
   b. $7,000
   c. $8,000
   d. $4,000

71. What is Holly's new boyfriend's name?

72. On what day does Michael donate blood?
   a. Valentine's Day
   b. Halloween
   c. Christmas
   d. Fourth of July

73. Who tries to steal cookies from the blood donation truck?

74. Who steals a bag of blood from the blood donation truck?

75. Who won the golden tickets?
   a. Red Cross
   b. Blue Cross
   c. Cumberland Mills
   d. Prestige

76. How many golden tickets does the winner find in their shipment?
    a. 8
    b. 10
    c. 5
    d. 4

77. Michael was planning what type of party when Charles Miner shows up for the first time at the Scranton office?

78. What shape are the bagels that Michael brought in for Charles and the employees?

79. What does Michael say to David Wallace after he quits?

80. After Pam quits, who does Charles put in her place temporarily?
    a. Kevin
    b. Ryan
    c. Oscar
    d. Angela

81. What is Andy's extension?
    a. 138
    b. 132
    c. 134
    d. 144

82. What sport does Andy pretend to like to impress Charles?

83. What soccer team was Jim on from second to fourth grade?
    a. The Red Team
    b. The Green Team
    c. The Orange Team
    d. The Purple Team

84. What does the caution sign on the wall next to the shower in Michael's new office say?
    a. Danger: Do Not Touch
    b. Caution: Hot Water
    c. Caution: Hot Water. Do Not Touch
    d. Danger: Hot Water

85. What is Erin's real first name?

86. What is the name of the ghost that haunts the office building, according to Dwight?
    a. Maggie
    b. Maddie
    c. Haddie
    d. Betty

87. Who made the first sale for The Michael Scott Paper Company?

88. What is the first name of The Michael Scott Paper Company's first client?
    a. Peter
    b. Kyle
    c. Russell
    d. Robert

89. How much does David Wallace first offer The Michael Scott Paper Company to buy them out?
    a. $12,000
    b. $20,000
    c. $60,000
    d. $30,000

90. Who wears matching outfits on casual day?

91. Pam says if you don't do what when Michael is pretending to be a robot, he will just keep going all day?
    a. Yell at him
    b. Ignore him
    c. Take out his battery
    d. Pull his plug

92. What state do Pam and Jim plan on getting married in last minute, but then decide not to?

93. What is the name of Bob Vance's new assistant that Phyllis is jealous of?
    a. Sarah
    b. Kathy
    c. Jessica
    d. Michelle

94. Who has a dance off in Café Disco?

95.   Who does Dwight bring to the company picnic?
        a.   His best friend, Rolph
        b.   Mose
        c.   His new girlfriend
        d.   Zeke

96.   Who is Michael happy to see at the company picnic?

97.   Where did Dunder meet Mifflin?

98.   How did Robert Mifflin kill himself?

99.   Michael and Holly tell everyone which branch is closing?

100.   When do Pam and Jim find out that Pam is pregnant?

SEASON SIX

1. What type of box does Andy fall into when doing "Parkour!"?

2. Who does "Parkour" in the office?
    a. Andy, Dwight and Ryan
    b. Dwight, Michael and Andy
    c. Ryan, Michael and Andy
    d. Michael, Andy and Kevin

3. What were the name of the summer interns who everyone thought were dating?
    a. Eric and Megan
    b. Kacy and Allen
    c. Alec and Maggie
    d. Tracey and Mitch

4. Who do the summer interns see with Stanley at a club?

5. Who does Michael ask for advice about his Colonoscopy?

6. Which employees investigate Darryl for workers comp fraud?
    a. Toby and Kevin
    b. Toby and Ryan
    c. Dwight and Toby
    d. Dwight and Nate

7. Who did Dwight and Toby see carrying a bag of dog food in front of Darryl's house?

8. Who spread a bunch of rumors around the office to hide the fact that Stanley was cheating on his wife?

9. What type of cheese did Andy put on the "cheese platter" for David Wallace?
    a. String Cheese, Cheddar style spread and Blue Cheese dressing
    b. Firm Cheddar, Cheddar style spread, Parmesan and String Cheese
    c. Cheddar style spread, Parmesan and Blue Cheese dressing
    d. Firm Cheddar, Cheddar style spread, Parmesan and Blue Cheese dressing

10. What does Phyllis plan to give Pam and Jim as a wedding gift?
   a. Money
   b. Handmade mittens
   c. A Birdhouse
   d. A Card

11. Why didn't Jim and Pam register for wedding gifts?

12. What does Kevin write in the memo line of the check that he gives Pam?
   a. "To love's eternal glory"
   b. "Best wishes!"
   c. "Mrs. Pam Halpert"
   d. "Congratulations"

13. What does Dwight eat at his desk that makes Pam throw-up into her trash can?

14. Who does Stanley bring to Pam and Jim's wedding?

15. What city was Pam and Jim's wedding in?

16. What was the name of Pam's cousin that Dwight tells Michael about?
   a. Jody Beasley
   b. Jocelyn Webster
   c. Isabel Webster
   d. Isabel Beasley

17. What is Dwight's confirmation number at the hotel where everyone stayed for Pam and Jim's wedding?
   a. Romeo-Tango T748
   b. Tango-Alhpa T5495
   c. Romeo-Tango-G77746
   d. Alpha-Tango G33346

18. How many safes did Dwight ask for in his hotel room?
   a. 1
   b. 2
   c. 3
   d. 4

19. How many horses does Dwight have?
   a. 3
   b. 9 and three-quarters

c.   3 and three-quarters
d.   7

20.   What was the name of Dwight's device he invented to take meat from horses without killing them?
a.   "Burgers-to-go"
b.   "Burger Alive"
c.   "Burger-on-the-go"
d.   "Dwight Burgers"

21.   Why does Pam take Andy to the hospital?

22.   How did Andy get hurt?

23.   What was the flavor of the snack that Pam's mom gave Michael at the wedding?
a.   Peach
b.   Apricot
c.   Cherry
d.   Apple

24.   What is an "upper decker"?

25.   What is the last name of Michael's Italian insurance agent?
a.   Gotti
b.   Grotti
c.   Gretti
d.   Gratti

26.   Where do Pam and Jim go on their honeymoon?
a.   Puerto Rico
b.   The Bahamas
c.   Costa Rica
d.   Bermuda

27.   What does Andy pretend to be during Michael's lunch meeting with his insurance agent?

28.   What does Andy say his first name is during Michael's lunch meeting with his insurance agent?
a.   John
b.   Mikey
c.   Pat
d.   Phil

29. Pam and Jim met Frank and Benny on their honeymoon and then refer to them as who?

30. Who is Michael's blind guy character that he made up?

31. What type of candy does Pam bring back from their honeymoon?
    a. White Chocolate
    b. Rum Candy
    c. Coco Leche
    d. Chocolate covered strawberries

32. What does Michael kill when he falls into the pond?

33. What type of authentic New York bagel does Dwight bring Stanley?
    a. Onion
    b. "Everything" bagel
    c. Gluten-free bagel
    d. Pumpernickel

34. What does Michael give Helene for her birthday?

35. Why does Michael break up with Helene?

36. How old does Helene turn on her birthday?

37. What is "Tub City"?

38. What is the name of the murder mystery game that Michael has the office play?
    a. "Buddies, Bourbon and Bullets"
    b. "Bells, Bourbon and Bullets"
    c. "Belles, Bourbon and Bullets"
    d. "Gals, Bourbon and Bullets"

39. What was the name of Angela's character in the murder mystery game?

40. What was the name of Erin's character in the murder mystery game?
    a. "Naughty Mellie"
    b. "Naughty Nellie Nutmeg"
    c. "Nutmeg Nellie"
    d. "Nutmeg Belle"

41. What was the name of Michael's character in the murder mystery game?
    a. "Caleb Crawdad"
    b. "Crawdad Carl"
    c. "Caleb Carl"
    d. "Crawdad Eddie"

42. What character does Dwight play on Earth day?

43. Who is Alan Brand?
    a. CEO of HB Heating and Air
    b. CEO of Dunder Mifflin
    c. CEO of Destroykits Unlimited
    d. There is no one by that name on the show

44. Who started the rumor that Jim is not "as in charge" as Michael is?
    a. Kevin
    b. Oscar
    c. Dwight
    d. Ryan

45. What does Michael say after Andy compliments him on his Elvis voice?

46. True or False: Jim is the first person to win employee of the month.

47. What did Michael promise to a group of third graders?

48. What room did Scott's Tots name after Michael at their high school?
    a. "The Michael Gary Scott Auditorium"
    b. "The Michael Scott Computer Lab"
    c. "The Michael Gary Scott Reading Room"
    d. "The Michael Scott Library"

49. What does Michael give the students of Scott's Tots when he goes to visit them?

50. What does Andy give Erin for her Secret Santa?

51. Who wanted to be Santa in season 6?
    a. Phyllis
    b. Kevin
    c. Toby
    d. Dwight

52. Who does Oscar have a crush on from the warehouse?
    a. Matt
    b. Kyle
    c. Nick
    d. Alex

53. Who is Dunder Mifflin sold to?

54. What is the name of the investment banker from Sabre who visits the Scranton office?
    a. Kenny Ward
    b. Eric Ward
    c. Micky Ward
    d. Nathan Ward

55. Who is the creator of "Computron"?

56. Who does Pam slap across the face in the parking lot?

57. What was in the box that was meant for Gabe that was delivered to the Scranton office?
    a. A printer and scanner
    b. A copier and printer
    c. A printer, a fax machine and a scanner
    d. A scanner, copier and fax machine

58. What does Michael leave inside Gabe's package after the employees put it back together?

59. What does Dwight make for Gabe when he arrives at the Scranton office for the first time?
    a. Scranton Hot Dogs from Scranton
    b. New York Hot Dogs from New York
    c. Ham and cheese sandwiches
    d. Peanut Butter and Jelly sandwiches

60. Who sings a song about Sabre?

61. Why did Michael book a room in Vancouver?
    a. To go see a friend
    b. To see new places
    c. To go to the Olympics
    d. To go to a business conference

62.   What is the first and last name of the CEO of Sabre?

63.   What type of Dog's does the CEO of Sabre have?
        a.   Mastiffs
        b.   Newfoundlands
        c.   Great Danes
        d.   German Shepherds

64.   Dwight says he will only stand for who when they enter a room?
        a.   The president
        b.   The president and Judge Judy
        c.   The president and his father
        d.   Dwight doesn't stand for anyone who walks in a room

65.   Who does Dwight decide to have a baby with?

66.   True or False: Pam and Kevin's last dinner before she goes on maternity leave was called, "Ultra-Eats".

67.   Who offers to drive Pam to the hospital because he has a Class "C" Driver's License?
        a.   Kevin
        b.   Michael
        c.   Toby
        d.   Dwight

68.   Why doesn't Pam want to go to the hospital?

69.   What is the full name of Jim and Pam's new baby?
        a.   Cecilia Marie Halbert
        b.   Cecilia Pamela Halbert
        c.   Cecilia Helene Halbert
        d.   Cecilia Catherine Halbert

70.   How much did Jim and Pam's baby weigh when she was born?
        a.   9lbs 10 oz
        b.   7 lbs 2 oz
        c.   7 lbs 3 oz
        d.   9 lbs 2 oz

71.   Who does Michael try to set up Erin with?

72.   What does Dwight find in Pam and Jim's kitchen?

73. What type of candy does Erin put on her desk for the employees for Saint Patrick's Day?
   a. Green Skittles
   b. Green apple candies
   c. Green M&M's
   d. Nothing

74. What did Dwight do with Jim's desk when Jim was gone with Pam on maternity leave?

75. What does Michael give Jo as a goodbye present when she leaves the office after visiting?

76. Who is at Erin's house when Andy goes to visit her when she's sick?
   a. Her foster brother named, Reed
   b. Her stepbrother named, Kyle
   c. Her foster brother named, Kaleb
   d. Her foster sister named, Lisa

77. Who does Michael give the expensive leads to?
   a. Angela, Toby and Kevin
   b. Angela, Kevin and Meredith
   c. Angela, Creed and Meredith
   d. Angela and Meredith

78. Michael gives Jim leads that have what on them?
   a. Riddles
   b. Nothing, they are blank
   c. Names of potential clients
   d. He never gives Jim any leads

79. Where do Dwight and Michael go look for the leads that were lost?

80. Who goes with Andy to look for the leads that were lost?
   a. Angela
   b. Dwight
   c. Erin
   d. Michael

81. Who does Michael turn into on his date with Pam's friend?

82. Stanley does how many push-ups to go home early?
    a.   23
    b.   27
    c.   30
    d.   25

83. How many push-ups does Jim do in the office?
    a.   19
    b.   15
    c.   10
    d.   14

84. What blood type is Isabel?
    a.   O positive
    b.   O negative
    c.   AB positive
    d.   AB negative

85. Who makes the cookie monster movie making fun of Kevin?

86. Who gets suspended for making fun of Kevin?
    a.   Jim, Pam and Dwight
    b.   Jim and Pam
    c.   Dwight and Jim
    d.   Jim, Dwight and Phyllis

87. What does Andy do for Erin on Secretary's day?
    a.   Has a party for her
    b.   Nothing
    c.   Gives her flowers
    d.   Takes her to lunch

88. What does Dwight give Erin for Secretary's day?
    a.   Nothing
    b.   A card
    c.   A barrel of beets
    d.   Beet Juice

89. What was the name of the married women that had an affair with Michael?
    a.   Diane
    b.   Diana
    c.   Donna
    d.   Deanna

90.   Who wins the placement for the minorities training program?

91.   What is the name of the minority training program?
    a.   Printing in Colors
    b.   Print in All Colors
    c.   Printing with Color
    d.   Colorful Prints

92.   Whose hand does Michael eat a mint out of?

93.   Who studied Morse code to prank Dwight?

94.   Who proves to Michael that Donna is cheating?
    a.   Pam
    b.   Phyllis
    c.   Andy
    d.   Jim

95.   True or False: Kevin makes a video of the Sabre printers catching on fire.

96.   Where does Dwight follow Donna to?

97.   Who eats mayo and black olives as comfort food?

98.   What type of kits does Toby leave around the office?
    a.   Radon
    b.   Radar
    c.   Mouse trap kits
    d.   Ant trap kits

99.   Michael keeps thinking the kits are what?

100.   Who was the whistleblower regarding the fire hazard of the Sabre printers?
    a.   Kevin
    b.   Dwight
    c.   Andy
    d.   Michael

SEASON SEVEN

1. What is the name of Michael's nephew who he hires to work in the office?
    a. Larry
    b. Lester
    c. Leo
    d. Luke

2. What does Michael's nephew call Andy instead of the Nard Dog?

3. What type of chips does Luke buy for the ice cream party?

4. Who does Michael spank in the office?

5. What clown poster is inside Dwight's "daycare center"?

6. True or False: Dwight tells everyone to boycott "The Stevenson Mall".

7. Why did the salesperson think there was blood all over Dwight's hands?

8. Who gives Michael a counseling session in the office?
    a. Toby
    b. Ryan
    c. Kevin
    d. Creed

9. What series did Michael reenact for his Sweeny Todd audition?
    a. Friends
    b. Law and Order
    c. NCIS
    d. The Young and the Restless

10. What does Michael drink while at the Sweeny Todd play?
    a. Water
    b. Juice
    c. Wine
    d. Soda

11.   True or False: Darryl's plumber plays the role of Sweeny Todd.

12.   What is the reason why Angela and Dwight use a punch card every time they have sex?

13.   Who babysat CeCe so Pam and Jim could go to Andy's play?
      a.   Angela
      b.   Erin
      c.   Helene
      d.   Pam's sister

14.   What does Nate use on the beehive?

15.   What does Michael get on his face that he thinks is Herpes?
      a.   A Pimple
      b.   An Ingrown hair
      c.   A Cut
      d.   He really does have Herpes

16.   Who is the first woman that Michael calls to tell that he has Herpes?
      a.   Donna
      b.   Holly
      c.   Helene
      d.   Carol

17.   What is the name of the salesman that Pam briefly dated?
      a.   Danny Tyler
      b.   Danny Corelle
      c.   Danny Cordray
      d.   Danny Tisdale

18.   Where did Danny Cordray work before Michael hired him as a traveling salesman?
      a.   Prestige Paper
      b.   Prince Paper
      c.   Osprey Paper
      d.   He was self employed

19.   Who plays drums in Darryl and Andy's jam sessions?

20.   What celebrity has the same bike model as Oscar?
      a.   Lance Bass
      b.   Lance Armstrong

c. Larry King
d. Leonardo DiCaprio

21. Who does Kevin dress up like for Halloween in Season 7?
    a. A penguin
    b. Michael Jackson
    c. Michael Moore
    d. A gorilla

22. True or False: The coupon book Pam chooses to be the prize for the Halloween costume winner is, "The 2011 Scranton/Wilkes-Barre Coupon Book."

23. How much is the coupon book worth?
    a. $5,000 in savings
    b. $10,00 in savings
    c. $15,000 in savings
    d. $12,000 in savings

24. Who wins the costume contest?
    a. Andy
    b. Oscar
    c. Toby
    d. Angela

25. Why does Dwight let everyone sneeze in his face and food?

26. What does Dwight give out at the entrance of the church at CeCe's christening?
    a. Flowers
    b. Rosaries
    c. His business cards
    d. Programs

27. What happens to CeCe's christening outfit?

28. What does Jim call the lady who was upset about the lack of scones and cider at CeCe's christening reception?
    a. "Sconsey Lady"
    b. "Cider Lady"
    c. "Sconsey Cider"
    d. "Sconsey"

29. What TV show does everyone watch at Gabe's apartment party?

30. True or False: Andy drinks powdered Sea Horses from Gabe's bedroom and it makes him sick.

31. What type of posters does Gabe have in his living room?
   a. French Art
   b. Japanese Art
   c. French Ads
   d. Chinese Ads

32. What did Jim do to cause everyone to miss "Blinded by the Light" on Glee?
   a. He changed the channel to check the scores of a sports game
   b. He made the power go out
   c. He cut the cable cord
   d. He turned the TV off

33. What was Dwight's hay maze called?

34. What was the password that the IT guy made up that offended Pam?
   a. Boobies
   b. Big Boobz
   c. Poop
   d. Booty

35. Why does Washington University want to "buy" WUPHF?

36. What was the senator's son eating when they met Angela for the first time?
   a. A lollipop
   b. A popsicle
   c. Cotton candy
   d. A candy apple

37. What is the name of Dwight's coffee shop in the lobby of the Dunder Mifflin building?
   a. "Dwight's Café"
   b. "Dwight's Caffeine Craze"
   c. "Dwight's Caffeine Corner"
   d. "Dwight's Office Cafe"

38. What does Darryl say "BTB" stands for when he texts girls?
    a. "Bring That Booty"
    b. "Bring The Beer"
    c. "Bring That Bourbon"
    d. "Bring The Bass"

39. What country was Michael talking about when he knew more than Oscar?

40. What type of lights does Dwight put in the office to save money?
    a. LED Lights
    b. Motion Sensor Lights
    c. Less lighting
    d. Candlelight

41. What is Oscar's nickname around the office because he is a "know-it-all"?

42. Dwight uses his feet to try and drink what type of beverage?
    a. Beet Juice
    b. Apple Juice
    c. Tea
    d. Coffee

43. Andy texted Darryl to come to the parking lot to watch what type of birds eat a melting ice cream cone on the ground?

44. What job title does Pam make up for herself?

45. What committee did Pam get rid of when she became Office Administrator?

46. What gift did Kelly give all the Scranton employees for Christmas?
    a. Flowers
    b. Pens
    c. A Hello Kitty Laptop sleeve
    d. Notebooks

47. What type of fight do Dwight and Jim get into because Dwight makes fun of Jim for commenting about it starting to snow?

48. True or False: Angela's new boyfriend is a member of congress.

49. Where in the office does Toby announce he will be a juror on the Scranton Strangler case?

a. In his cubical
b. Over the phone
c. In the conference room
d. In Michael's office

50. Why does Michael destroy Holly's toy?

51. What is Darryl's daughter's name?
a. Jayla
b. Jules
c. Jada
d. Jade

52. What is the name of Dwight's volunteer crime patrolling club?
a. "Armored Knights"
b. "Knights of the Night"
c. "Knights who Fight"
d. "Knights of Scranton"

53. What is the name of the strip club that Dwight went into with his roller skates on?

54. True or False: Darryl was referring to strippers who "work the day shift on Monday at noon" when he tells Andy, "You can't unsee that."

55. What band does Andy request the DJ to play when he is roller skating at the roller skate rink?

56. What is Creed's New Year's Resolution?
a. Stop drinking
b. Do a cartwheel
c. Get a new job
d. Start working out

57. What is the name of Michael's Greek character that he plays at Andy's small business seminar?
a. Mikanos
b. Mikonos
c. Milkonos
d. Makanos

58. Where does Jim leave Michael while Michael is using the restroom?

59. What does "A.P.B." stand for?
    a. "Always Put Behind"
    b. "Ask Pam Beasley"
    c. "Ask Pam's Buddy"
    d. "Always Play Ball"

60. What type of restaurant does Michael try to dine and dash?
    a. Italian
    b. Greek
    c. Chinese
    d. Mexican

61. Who sings Erin's Valentine clue, "The Temp at Night"?
    a. Andy
    b. Gabe
    c. Ryan
    d. Michael

62. True or False: Frank is the security guard for the Dunder Mifflin building.

63. True or False: Erin's final valentine's day clue from Gabe is a rose.

64. Who is the main character in "Threat Level Midnight"?

65. How long did it take Michael to complete "Threat Level Midnight"?
    a. 10 years
    b. 8 years
    c. 7 years
    d. 4 years

66. What does Cherokee Jack have Michael Scarn use on the ice to get better at hockey?

67. Who does Michael Scarn kill in the locker room?
    a. Golden Face
    b. Cherokee Jack
    c. Oscar
    d. The President

68. Jasmine Windsong is played by who?

69. What does Jasmine Windsong sing backwards to give Michael Scarn a clue?
   a. "The clues are under the stadium."
   b. "Golden face is under the stadium."
   c. "The hostages are under the stadium."
   d. "The fugitives are under the stadium."

70. What is Jasmine Windsong laying on when she dies?
   a. A table
   b. A bar
   c. A piano
   d. The floor

71. What does Michael say is "intregral" to the story of "Threat Level Midnight"?
   a. When Cherokee Jack dies
   b. When Goldenface dies
   c. When he kills Oscar
   d. When Toby gets shot in the head by Goldenface

72. Goldenface tells Michael Scarn the bomb is inside of what?
   a. The stadium
   b. A puck
   c. A box
   d. The president's office

73. Who plays the role of Michael Scarn's nurse?

74. What is the name of the bartender in "Threat Level Midnight?"
   a. Billy
   b. Benny
   c. Butch
   d. Bob

75. What does Karen ask Michael Scarn?

76. What number on the jukebox is Michael Scarn's "That's How You Do the Scarn" song?
   a. G-10
   b. G-7
   c. G-9
   d. G-4

77. Who plays the members of the bachelorette party in the bar in "Threat Level Midnight?"
    a.   Meredith, Phyllis and Karen
    b.   Meredith, Angela and Karen
    c.   Angela, Phyllis and Karen
    d.   Meredith, Angela, Phyllis and Karen

78. Who yells, "If doing the Scarn is gay, then I'm the biggest queer on earth!"?

79. What is the name of Michael's book on business?
    a.   "Manage Your Life"
    b.   "Somehow I Manage"
    c.   "Somehow They Manage"
    d.   "How to Manage"

80. What is the name of Michael's HBO Comedy Special that he dreams of creating?
    a.   "Here We Go Again, Dot, Dot, Dot"
    b.   "Here They Go Again, Dot, Dot, Dot"
    c.   "Here I Go Again, Dot, Dot, Dot"
    d.   "I'm Going Again, Dot, Dot, Dot"

81. What is Michael Scarn's hockey jersey number?
    a.   22
    b.   23
    c.   10
    d.   11

82. What is the team name on Michael Scarn's hockey jersey?
    a.   "Scarn Stars"
    b.   "Threat Level Midnight"
    c.   "All Star Scarns"
    d.   "All Stars"

83. What hockey item explodes in Goldenface's lap?

84. Who is the narrator in "Threat Level Midnight"?
    a.   Michael Scarn (voice of Stanley)
    b.   Michael Scarn (voice of Michael Scott)
    c.   Jim
    d.   Darryl

85.   True or False: Dwight and Jim trick Todd Packer into going to New York.

86.   What does Meredith trade Dwight for a tack?
        a.   Half used candle
        b.   A picture
        c.   Nothing
        d.   A Squid

87.   Ryan sells what two items at the garage sale?

88.   Phyllis is on the label for what food product?
        a.   Ryan's Salsa
        b.   Ryan's Pasta Sauce
        c.   Ryan's Pesto Sauce
        d.   Ryan's Ketchup

89.   What does Dwight trade Erin for a squid?
        a.   A tack
        b.   A penny
        c.   A book
        d.   A flashlight

90.   What is the name of Jim's legumes that Dwight traded a telescope for at the garage sale?
        a.   "Professor Copperfield's Miracle Legumes"
        b.   "Mister Copperfield's Miracle Legumes"
        c.   "Doctor Copperfield's Miracle Legumes"
        d.   "Professor Cooperton's Miracle Legumes"

91.   Andy, Kevin and Darryl play what game during the garage sale?

92.   Where does Dwight plant his legumes?
        a.   At his farm
        b.   In pots outside the office building near the warehouse
        c.   Inside the office in planters
        d.   He threw the legumes away

93.   What drink does Michael order at the bar when he goes to meet Angelo Vickers for the first time?
        a.   Water
        b.   Gin and Tonic
        c.   Kahlua Sombrero
        d.   Cranberry Juice and Vodka

94. How long did Michael work at Dunder Mifflin?
    a.   20 years
    b.   18 years
    c.   19 years
    d.   21 years

95. What city and state are Holly and Michael moving to?

96. When Kevin wears his new wig to the office on Angelo Vickers first day, what celebrity does he compare himself to?
    a.   Ben Stiller
    b.   Aston Kutcher
    c.   Bruce Willis
    d.   Brad Pitt

97. How many minutes did Michael work at Dunder Mifflin?
    a.   9,986,000 minutes
    b.   8,986,000 minutes
    c.   5,986,000 minutes
    d.   10,986,000 minutes

98. What does Dwight feed to Michael when Michael is sitting on the roof of the office building?
    a.   Meatballs
    b.   Bull testicles
    c.   Dog Testicles
    d.   Fish sticks

99. What toy does Michael let Angelo Vickers have?

100. What going away gift does Phyllis give to Michael?

101. What going away present does Michael give to Andy?

102. What going away present does Michael give to Oscar?

103. What is the name of Toby's brother who lives in Boulder?
    a.   Troy Flenderson
    b.   Roy Flenderson
    c.   Rory Flenderson
    d.   Tory Flenderson

104. What game does Michael play with Dwight before he leaves Scranton?

105. What time does Michael leave to the airport in Michael's goodbye episode?
    a.   5:00 PM
    b.   3:00PM
    c.   4:00PM
    d.   1:00 PM

106. What falls on Angelo Vickers in the warehouse?
    a.   A pallet
    b.   A basketball hoop
    c.   A case of paper
    d.   A ladder

107. How long was Dwight "acting manager"?
    a.   One day
    b.   Two weeks
    c.   5 days
    d.   One week

108. True or False: Dwight accidently shoots a Beaumont-Adams revolver inside the office.

109. When Creed is acting manager, he calls Dunder Mifflin "Great ___"?
    a.   "Great Mifflin"
    b.   "Great Dunder"
    c.   "Great Bratton"
    d.   "Great Creedland"

110. What acronym does Creed use during his meeting?

111. When first appearing on the show, which job position does Nellie apply for?
    a.   Special Events Planner
    b.   Special Projects Manager
    c.   Branch Manager
    d.   CFO

112. Dwight pretends to be a burn victim by the name of what?
    a.   Jacques Souvenier
    b.   Jack Souvenier
    c.   Jason Souvenier
    d.   Joshua Souvenier

113.   Who does Ryan think would make the best manager?
    a.   Nellie
    b.   A homeless person
    c.   Jim
    d.   No one

114.   Who gets the job as branch manager?

115.   What lake does Jim Carry say he snuck away from to go to the branch manager interview?

SEASON EIGHT

1. How many employees participated in "planking"?
    a. 9
    b. 4
    c. 10
    d. 6

2. Who does Robert California choose to be Branch Manager after convincing Jo to give him her job?
    a. Andy
    b. Dwight
    c. Kelly
    d. Jim

3. Name all the employees on the right side of Robert California's list in his notebook?

4. True or False: Gabe was on the right side of Robert California's list.

5. What is the name of the Sabre Tablet?
    a. The Home
    b. The Computron
    c. The Pyramid
    d. The C-Span

6. What type of Pizza does Andy order for the employees on the left side of Robert California's list?

7. What was the prize for the employees if they get to 5,000 points?
    a. A Vibrator
    b. Kids Toys
    c. Andy will get a tattoo on his butt
    d. Andy will wear a dress to work

8. What year did Andy graduate from Cornell University?
    a. 1993
    b. 1991
    c. 1995
    d. 1994

9. How much money did the warehouse workers win?

10. After not winning the lottery, Darryl eats what in his basement?

11. After all the warehouse workers quit, who crashes the forklift inside the warehouse?
    a. Darryl
    b. Dwight
    c. Andy
    d. Erin

12. What type of allergy does Darryl develops at 35 years old?
    a. Lactose
    b. Nut
    c. Soy
    d. Sulfite

13. Which employees were pictured on the billboards that were defaced?

14. True or False: Andy's Garden Party starts at 3:00PM.

15. True or False: Andy's parents at the garden party are different actors from the actors who were at Toby's goodbye party.

16. What was the name of Jim's book about how to throw garden parties?

17. What name did Jim use for the author of his book?
    a. Jimothy Smith
    b. James Trickington
    c. Michael Scarn
    d. James Trickster

18. How much did Dwight pay for Jim's book?
    a. $2.00
    b. $1.00
    c. $5.00
    d. $3.00

19. Who is Angela naming her son after?

20. What is Mose's job at the garden party?
   a. Waiter
   b. Cook
   c. The valet
   d. Musician

21. What item does Robert California bring to Andy's garden party as a gift?

22. What is Erin's Halloween costume in Season 8?
   a. Cat
   b. Puppy
   c. Wendy
   d. Monster

23. What is Robert California's son's name?

24. Who dresses up like Skelton's for Halloween in Season 8?

25. True or False: Kelly's worst fear is never marrying.

26. What does Creed dress up as for Halloween in Season 8?

27. What song does Andy snig at the end of every workday?

28. Who develops the accountability booster?
   a. Andy
   b. Jim
   c. Robert California
   d. Dwight

29. Who does Gabe develop a crush on?
   a. Angela
   b. Pam
   c. Val
   d. Kathy

30. True or False: Pam pretends to be in labor on multiple occasions.

31. What instrument does Robert California play when jamming with Kevin and the zits?

32. How many employees decide to attend Andy's trip to Gettysburg?
   a. 10
   b. 14
   c. 6
   d. 9

33. What do the hats that Andy made for the Gettysburg trip say?

34. True or False: The Battle of Schrute Farms was a true war battle.

35. What was Stanley's paper for women called and how was it spelled?

36. What type of flag does Andy bring to Gettysburg?

37. Kevin says, "Never trust a cookie with_____."
   a. A man's name
   b. A women's name
   c. A girl's name
   d. No name

38. What is Robert California's wife's name?

39. Ture or False: Robert California wants his wife to work at Dunder Mifflin.

40. What is the name of Dwight's gym that he opens in the office building?
   a. Dwight Schrute's Gym for Fitness
   b. Dwight Schrute's Gym for Men
   c. Dwight Schrute's Gym
   d. Dwight Schrute's Gym for Muscles

41. What is at the ripping station at Dwight's gym?

42. What type of Christmas does Stanley want?

43. Where does Andy buy Dwight for Christmas that is by the "Sea of Tranquility"?

44. What is Andy's "Gam Gam's" name?
   a. Rebecca
   b. Janice
   c. Ruth
   d. Denise

45. When does Andy first introduce Jessica to the office employees?
    a. At the office Christmas party
    b. On the Gettysburg trip
    c. At Robert California's house party
    d. At his house

46. What band is Robert California referring to when he says, "It's rock for people who don't like rock, its rap for people who don't like rap, it's pop for people who don't like pop."

47. What is Jessica's job and where does she work?
    a. Assistant Cross-Country Coach at Cornell University
    b. Cheerleading Coach at Scranton College
    c. Cheerleading Coach at Scranton High School
    d. Assistant Cross-Country Coach at Bryn Mawr

48. Why do the warehouse workers call the office workers "Popsicles"?

49. When Dwight steals Jim's credit card number, what does he buy?

50. True or False: Dwight's porcupine's name is Harrieta.

51. What was the longest silent streak in office history?
    a. 14 minutes
    b. 25 minutes
    c. 15 minutes
    d. 12 minutes

52. What does Kevin say that breaks the silence during the office's silent steak?

53. What is the name of the trivia contest that Oscar attends?
    a. Triviocity
    b. Triviocalypse
    c. Trividelphia
    d. Trivimania

54. How much money will the winner of the trivia contest win?

55. What household appliance does Gabe compare himself to?

56. What team wins the trivia contest?

57. True or False: Erin flirts with Dwight to try to make Andy jealous.

58. How many bottles of wine does Robert California have in his wine cellar?
    a. 450
    b. 300
    c. 1200
    d. 1100

59. What wine does Toby pick from Robert California's wine cellar?
    a. 1995 Bordeaux Chateau
    b. 1992 Chateau Margaux
    c. 1995 Chateau Margaux
    d. 1992 Bordeaux Chateau

60. What song does Andy dance to when relieving stress in the warehouse?
    a. "Footloose" by Kenny Loggins
    b. "Footloose" by Kenny Rogers
    c. "Hard Day's Night" by The Beatles
    d. "Gonna Make you Sweat" by C+C Factory

61. True or False: Jim was on a jury for a hit and run trail.

62. What food truck did Toby eat from every day when he was on the jury for the Scranton Strangler?

63. What type of food did toby always order from the food truck during his jury duty?
    a. Burritos
    b. Empanadas
    c. Taquitos
    d. Enchiladas

64. Who figures out that Jim was lying about being on jury duty?

65. Who translates for Ernesto?
    a. Nate
    b. Ernesto's co-worker
    c. Toby
    d. Ernesto's son

66. Who says, "well, usually I'm a burrito guy, but if you won't tell I won't. Wink, wink."
    a. Jim
    b. Andy
    c. Creed
    d. Oscar

67. How much did Angela's baby weigh at birth?
    a. 9 pounds, 6 ounces
    b. 8 pounds 7 ounces
    c. 9 pounds 7 ounces
    d. 10 pounds 2 ounces

68. What procedure does Dwight tell the nurse in the office to cancel when he figures out, he could potentially be Phillip's father?

69. True or False: Kevin is allergic to walnuts.

70. What day does Pam come back to work from maternity leave?

71. What word does the Schrute family use when everything in a man's life comes together perfectly?

72. Nam all the employees who go to Tallahassee to open the Sabre store with Dwight?

73. What is Kathy's hotel room number when she travels to Tallahassee?
    a. 234
    b. 243
    c. 211
    d. 278

74. Name the two sentences that Jim wrote on his hotel wall to scare Dwight?

75. What is the name of the cashier in the gift shop in the hotel where Dwight purchases antacids and a gift for Phillip?
    a. Sarah
    b. Michelle
    c. Heather
    d. Melissa

76. Who is President of Special Projects for Sabre?

77. What magazine does Creed start reading after Andy puts new magazines out for the employees?
    a. Dwell
    b. Sports Illustrated
    c. Sports Trading
    d. Cosmopolitan

78. True or False: Dwight defines the "Three Pillars of Retail".

79. What are "Anderson's Three Pillars of Retail?"
    a. Convenience, Service, Building Loyalty
    b. Service, Dedication, Honesty
    c. Building Loyalty, Honesty, Service
    d. Dedication, Service, Sales

80. What is the name of Oscar's dog?
    a. Rover
    b. Daisy
    c. Gerald
    d. Sparky

81. What breakfast food does Erin try to order at the hotel but they don't have?

82. What is Val's boyfriend's name?

83. How old are the mattresses at Schrute Farms?
    a. 100 years old
    b. 50 years old
    c. 200 years old
    d. 75 years old

84. True or False: Gabe's full name is Gabriel Susan Lewis.

85. What name does Erin use when she camps outside of the Sabre store as a "hipster"?

86. What town was Nellie born in?
    a. London
    b. Basildon
    c. Bakewell
    d. Southwold

87. Which Spice Girl did Nellie audition for?

88. According to Toby, what three things should the employees do if they are attacked?

89. What is the name of the girl who punches Andy in the face?

90. What color sports drink does Ryan want Jim to get him?

91. What is Erin's favorite food?
    a. Spaghetti
    b. Lasagna
    c. Eggplant Parmesan
    d. Fettuccine Alfredo

92. Who's bachelorrete party do Erin and Andy stop by to see Jessica?

93. Ryan thinks what musician died and gets upset?

94. The office employees attend a silent auction for what society?
    a. The Scranton Dog Welfare Society
    b. The Scranton Animal Welfare Society
    c. The Scranton Pet Welfare Society
    d. The Scranton Animal Rescue Society

95. How much does Dwight accidently donate at the silent auction?

96. What paper company name does Andy make up get the CEO of Prestige Direct Mail Solutions to do business with him?

97. Who is Lloyd Gross?

98. What does Dwight take from the trash to have tested to determine if he is the father of Angela's baby?

99. Robert California tells David Wallace his name is what?

    b.	Mike California
    c.	Robert Ventura
    d.	Bob Kazamakis

100.	What is the flavor of the Asian energy drink that Darryl tries?

SEASON NINE

1. What is Dwight's power drink made from?
   a. Carrot juice
   b. Protein powder
   c. Beet run-off
   d. Celery root

2. Ture of False: Dwight found out he was the father of Angela's baby at the paternity testing center.

3. Where did Kelly and her fiancé, Ravi, move to?

4. Ravi became what type of professor at a university?

5. Who creates "The Chore Wheel"?

6. Which chore was not on the chore wheel?
   a. Empty Trash
   b. Dust copier machines
   c. Water plants
   d. Clean annex

7. What time is Roy's wedding with his new fiancé?

8. What is the name of Nellie's big charity initiative?
   a. "Operation: Give Back"
   b. "Operation: Initiating Giving Back"
   c. "Operation: Giving Back"
   d. "Operation: Dunder Mifflin Give Back"

9. What charity does Stanley pick for Nellie's charity initiative?

10. What charity does Dwight pick for Nellie's charity initiative?

11. What is Roy's new fiancé's name?
    a. Laura
    b. Sarah
    c. Megan
    d. Emma

12. What is the name of Jim and Pam's Asian friend who pretends to be Jim to prank Dwight?

13. What language does Dwight teach Erin?

14. True or False: Phyllis' great-great grandmother was responsible for spreading Cholera to the United States.

15. What warehouse employee passed away in Season 9?
    a. Mike
    b. Carl
    c. Jerry
    d. Frank

16. What happened in the office that was caused by a concentration of wiring in one area?
    a. EMH Hotspots
    b. EMF Hotspots
    c. EHF Hotspots
    d. EMS Hotspots

17. Why does Nellie ask Andy to write her a character reference?

18. The office employees take the work bus to what pie place?
    a. "Laverne's Pies, Tires Fixed Also"
    b. "Laverne's Pies, Cars Fixed Also"
    c. "Laverne's Pies and Tire Service"
    d. "Laverne's Pies and Car Service"

19. What does Kevin call Oscar to make him smash his pie into his face?

20. What gets stuck on Dwight's head?

21. What does Andy dress up like for Halloween in Season 9?

22. What is the first song that "Here Comes Treble" sings when they arrive at the office?

23. What was Andy's signature song when he was in "Here Comes Treble"?

24. How much money does Jim invest into "Athlead"?
    a. $40,000
    b. $100,000
    c. $10,000
    d. $20,000

25. What was the name of the medication that Dwight found on the floor inside the office?
    a. Wellburtin
    b. Zanax
    c. Dematril
    d. Dumatril

26. What does Nellie dress up like for Halloween in Season 9?

27. Who steals Andy's nickname, "Boner Champ"?

28. How did Andy get the nickname, "Boner Champ?"

29. Who dresses up like Charlie Brown for Halloween in Season 9?
    a. Oscar
    b. Kevin
    c. Creed
    d. Toby

30. Dwight thinks he is having an interview with what radio host?

31. What is the name of the radio show that Dwight thinks he is being interviewed on?

32. What type of boat does Andy's family own?
    a. 43 Foot-17th Century Ketch
    b. 42-Foot Artic Schooner
    c. 43-Foot Tartan Sloop
    d. 42-Foot Dinghy

33. Nellie pretends to be which radio host?

34. Where did Andy's father run off to with a younger woman?

35. Who does Andy find trapped inside a room on his family's boat?

36. Where does Andy sail his family's boat to?
    a.   Bermuda
    b.   The Bahamas
    c.   Barbados
    d.   Bahrain

37. What does Andy have on his boat to purify ocean water?
    a.   Desalinating Device
    b.   Purification Tablets
    c.   Boiling device
    d.   Chlorine Tablets

38. What does Dwight refer to as, "The White Whale", in the paper industry?

39. Who called Gina Rogers at Apex Technology "Gy-na" during an entire sales meeting?

40. Men in the office participated in "Movember" for what type of charity?

41. True or False: Jan's new assistant is named Megan.

42. Dwight tells Pam Jan's new assistant's license plate number was what?
    a.   415-YCL
    b.   425-STL
    c.   415-YTL
    d.   425-LCY

43. Meredith calls Pam, "Queen of the ___", when Pam is painting the mural in the warehouse.

44. Who does Jim ask to cover for him while he is working in Philadelphia?

45. Angela hires Trevor to do what to Oscar?

46. What company does Pam call to get a complaint filed against her?
    a.   Heymont Brake and Tire
    b.   Montrose Tires and Service
    c.   Heymont Car Service
    d.   Montrose Car Care

47. Who thinks jazz is stupid?
    a.   Angela and Pam
    b.   Dwight and Angela

c.   Stanley and Phyllis
d.   Jim and Pam

48.   True or False: Angela tells Toby that gayness "comes from breast feeding".

49.   Who asks Toby, "What is Red Vining"?
a.   Kevin
b.   Kevin and Stanley
c.   Dwight and Angela
d.   Erin

50.   In the opening scene in Season 9, Episode 9, what does the mug on Jim's desk say?
a.   "Impish or Admirable?"
b.   "Grandma is the best"
c.   "Belsnickel is here"
d.   "Grandma is a Great Cook"

51.   Who recommends having an authentic Pennsylvania Dutch Christmas for the office Christmas party?

52.   Who is Saint Nicolas' Rural German Companion?

53.   What is Gluwhein?
a.   It is also known as "Glow-wine"
b.   Used to sterilize medical instruments
c.   Part of the authentic Pennsylvania Dutch Christmas
d.   All of the Above

54.   What is Hog Maw?
a.   Stuffed pig stomach
b.   Stuffed sheep stomach
c.   Stuffed cow's stomach
d.   Stuffed horse stomach

55.   Who is Belsnickel's side kick?
a.   Zwarte Piet
b.   Belspiet
c.   Hasenpfeffer
d.   Belsnickette

56.   Was Phyllis determined to be admirable or impish by Belsnickel?

57. Who says Meredith is kind of cute and has an "Emma Stone thing going on"?

58. Who breaks the pig rib?

59. Who broke off the bigger half of the pig rib?

60. True or False: Nellie kisses Toby.

61. Who brought lice into the office?

62. Dwight said the kids in school called him what names because he had lice?
    a. "Girl Puncher", "Freak"
    b. "Freak", "Four Eyes, "Sci-Fi Nerd, "Girl Puncher"
    c. "Freak", "Girl Puncher", "Four Eyes"
    d. "Lice Head", "Girl Puncher", "Freak", "Idiot"

63. Name the people who did not get lice in the office on the day it was brought into the office?
    a. Nellie, Kevin, Pete, Phyllis, Erin
    b. Nellie, Erin, Darryl, Phyllis, Pete
    c. Nellie, Kevin, Darryl, Phyllis, Dwight
    d. Nellie, Kevin, Darryl, Oscar, Creed

64. What type of animal did Clark compare Jan to?
    a. A swarm of bees
    b. A Cougar
    c. A Lion
    d. A Tiger

65. True or False: The first time Erin ever tried espresso was in Season 9.

66. True or False: The first time Oscar finds out there is hardwood flooring under the carpet in the office is in Season 9 when the copier rips the carpet.

67. Who goes with Darryl to his interview in Philadelphia at Jim's new company?

68. What did Pam find out in the middle of CeCe's dance recital?

69. Who threw a milkshake into the window of a drive-thru?
    a. Dwight
    b. Darryl
    c. Nellie

d.   Erin

70.   What company did Jim's company lose as an investor?
     a.   Bridgeport Capital
     b.   Brookings Point Investments
     c.   BridgeWest Investments
     d.   BridgeBrook Capital

71.   Who comforts Pam after Jim got upset at her for failing to record CeCe's dance recital?

72.   Who protected Pam from Frank?

73.   True or False. Mose interviews to be a sales associate at Dunder Mifflin.

74.   What school did Dwight go to as a child?
     a.   Flight school
     b.   X-men school
     c.   Superman college
     d.   Batman school

75.   What does Erin name the bear she puts in Darryl's office when they are being "sneaky sneaks"?

76.   Who draws butts all over Pam's mural?

77.   What nationality is Robert Lipton's gardener?
     a.   Mexican
     b.   Spanish
     c.   Malaysian
     d.   German

78.   Which employees put paint on Frank's truck?

79.   Why did Brian get fired?

80.   What does Kevin call the rotten milk Andy left in the fridge?
     a.   "Chunky Tasty Milk"
     b.   "Chunky Lemon Milk"
     c.   "Chunky Yummy Milk"
     d.   "Chunky Rotten Milk"

81. What does the pedicurist call Clark?
    a. "A Pretty Girl"
    b. "Sexy"
    c. "Ugly"
    d. "Fake boyfriend"

82. What huge account did Andy lose when he got back from his boat trip?

83. How does David Wallace find out Andy was gone for 3 months?

84. How does Dwight usually clean up his Aunty Shirley?

85. Who gets the red dirt thrown in their face by Dwight?

86. What type of vehicle is Jeb driving when he shows up to Aunt Shirley's funeral?
    a. Red Corvette
    b. Red Toyota Prius
    c. Red Ford Mustang
    d. Red Chevy Truck

87. When Todd Packer shows up at the office, what bakery does he say his cupcakes are from?

88. Who doesn't end up eating one of Todd Packer's cupcakes?

89. What is the first name of Ester's father?
    a. Henry
    b. Fred
    c. Carl
    d. Zeke

90. What does Dwight place in front of Ester when they are playing music on his porch?

91. What audio book does Phyllis listen to in the office?

92. Who pours water on Phyllis to make her stop listening to her audio book?

93. Who else gets a bucket of water thrown on them?

94. In the Dutch version of the office promos, what is Kevin referred to as?
    a. "Skrald Mand" ("Dumpster Man")
    b. "Bruto" ("Gross")
    c. "Bruto Gewicht ("Gross Weight")
    d. "Vet Mand" ("Fat Man")

95. Who was referred to as "Cloken Tre Pige" (The 3PM Girl) in the Dutch promo?
    a. Erin
    b. Pam
    c. Angela
    d. Meredith

96. What does Stanley drink while making his way up the staircase during Stairmageddon?

97. What is in Stanley's drink that Pete refers to as a "Morning 3x5"?

98. What is the name of Andy's first "movie" that his agent books for him?
    a. "HRPDC Chemical Protocols Procedures"
    b. "HRPDC Chemical Handling Protocols"
    c. "HPPC Chemical Handling Protocols
    d. "HRPDD Chemical Safety and Handling"

99. Where is Dwight's black belt ceremony?

100. What is Andy's guitar's name?
    a. Lorelei
    b. Lora
    c. Lilly
    d. Lillia

101. Where did Dwight get the new security door for the office?

102. What does A.A.R.M stand for?

103. What was the name of the television competition show that Andy tried out for?

104. Casey Dean was from what city and state?
    a.   Philadelphia, Pennsylvania
    b.   Cincinnati, Ohio
    c.   Scranton, Pennsylvania
    d.   Chicago, Illinois

105. At the television singing competition, Andy dresses up like an old man and says his name is what?
    a.   Travis Cornell
    b.   Russell Cornell
    c.   Ezra Cornell
    d.   David Cornell

106. What political position does Oscar run for?

107. What was the name of the band that Creed was in in the 1960's?

108. Who stole weapons-grade LSD from the military?
    a.   Kevin
    b.   Creed
    c.   Todd Packer
    d.   Toby

109. Who what does Bestisch Mensch mean?

110. What was Kevin's magic number called?

111. What is Angela's big sister's name?

112. True or False: Meredith's son is a male stripper.

113. For the first seven years of the office documentary, Meredith was getting what type of college degree?

114. Why does Dwight fire Jim and Pam?

115. Who said, "I wish there was a way to know you're in the good old days before you've actually left them."

116. What type of car is Dwight driving in the opening scene of the "Finale" episode?

117. What channel is The Office documentary aired on?
    a.   PBS
    b.   ABC
    c.   FX
    d.   HBO

118. In the "finale" episode, the camera crew says they came back to get more footage for what?
    a.   A DVD
    b.   No reason
    c.   To see how much paper they have sold since the documentary aired
    d.   They never said why

119. How does Dwight tell Kevin he is fired?

120. True or False: Dwight hires Devon back to work in the office.

121. Dwight and Jim have known each other for how many years?
    a.   13 years
    b.   15 years
    c.   12 years
    d.   10 years

122. Where does Nellie say she moved to after the documentary aired?
    a.   Iceland
    b.   England
    c.   Poland
    d.   Ireland

123. Where did Toby move to after the documentary ended?

124. True or False: Andy changed his phone number after the documentary aired.

125. In the final scene of the series, Pam says, "There's a lot of beauty in _____ _____. Isn't that the point?"

BONUS QUESTIONS

1. True or False: Seth Rogan auditioned for the role of Dwight.

2. True or False: Some of the actors researched various paper companies to enhance their roles.

3. True or False: Phyllis was a casting agent for the show.

4. Who was the first actor to get a role on The Office?

5. Which cast member was an NFL cheerleader?

6. True or False: Angela originally auditioned for the role of Phyllis.

7. Which Parks and Recreation actress originally auditioned for the role of Jan on "The Office"?

8. True or False: Poor Richards is an actual bar in Scranton.

9. Which restaurant mentioned in the show was an actual restaurant in Scranton that had a food item named after Michael Scott?
   a. Farley's
   b. Chili's
   c. Benihanas
   d. Kelly's

10. Which actors interned for Conan O'Brien?
    a. Mindy Kaling
    b. Ellie Kemper
    c. John Krasinski
    d. All of the above

11. True or False: Froggy 101 is not an actual radio station in Scranton.

12. Which actor filmed parts of Scranton for the opening credits?
    a. John Krasinski
    b. Rainn Wilson
    c. Mindy Kaling
    d. B.J. Novak

13. Who had grandparents who were actual Polish beet framers?
    a. Brian Baumgartner
    b. Rainn Wilson
    c. Greg Daniels
    d. Paul Lieberstein

14. True or False: Jenna Fischer kept the engagement ring that Jim gave to Pam.

15. What office supplies store actually sold Dunder Mifflin brand office supplies and paper products?

16. John Krasinski had to wear a wig during what season because he shaved his head for a role on another show?

17. True or False: Angela Kinsey and Jenna Fischer are best friends in real life.

18. Paul Lieberstein and B.J. Novak have vacationed together where?
    a. Puerto Rico
    b. Costa Rica
    c. Spain
    d. Thailand

19. Who is Greg Daniels?

20. Which actors have the same actual first names as their characters on the show?
    a. Angela, Erin, Oscar and Creed
    b. Phyllis, Angela and Creed
    c. Angela, Creed, Oscar and Phyllis
    d. Creed, Daryll, Angela, Oscar and Toby

21. Which Office actor was married to Paul Leiberstein's brother?
    a. Phyllis
    b. Jenna
    c. Angela
    d. Rashida

22. Who is Paul Leiberstein's sister married to?
    a.   B.J. Novak
    b.   Greg Daniels
    c.   Oscar Nunez
    d.   Creed Bratton

23. True or False: Jim proposed to Pam at an actual gas station in Scranton.

24. Why did the writers of "The Office" choose Andy to be the next manager over Darryl?
    a.   Darryl was "too smart and rational"
    b.   Andy would cause more disasters
    c.   Andy was irrational and based his business decisions on his personal feelings instead of logic
    d.   All of the Above

25. True or False: The 1st season of The Office did very well and had many viewers.

26. Dunder Mifflin is an actual member of what?
    a.   Scranton Chamber of Commerce
    b.   Scranton Business Partners Committee
    c.   Office Supply Committee of Scranton
    d.   Better Business Bureau

27. The Office was initially going to be aired on what channel?
    a.   FX or HBO
    b.   Showtime
    c.   FOX
    d.   CW

28. Roy Anderson is played by which actor?
    a.   David Denman
    b.   Craig Robinson
    c.   David Parker
    d.   Andrew Miller

29. Why did Greg Daniels pick specific cities for the Dunder Mifflin branches?
   a. His family members reside in those cities
   b. He has always wanted to visit those cities
   c. He though the names of the cities were funny
   d. He just randomly picked them off a map

30. What year did the first episode of The Office air?

31. Mose's character was inspired by what?
   a. Greg Daniels' best friend
   b. A reality show about Amish people
   c. One of the writers of the show was raised in an Amish community
   d. He was inspired by a cartoon character on a television show

32. What was the name of the spin-off show that Dwight was supposed to star in?
   a. The Beets Motel
   b. The Life of a Beet Farmer
   c. The Farm
   d. Schrute Farms

33. True or False: John Krasinski's first on-screen kiss was with Jenna Fischer.

34. True or False: Production was shut down during the episode titled, "Lecture Circuit" because John Krasinski and Rainn Wilson couldn't stop laughing during the birthday party scene.

35. What season was Angela Kinsey actually pregnant in?

36. During the show's opening credits, the "Penn Paper Building" is shown. The building was then across the street from a bar named what?
   a. Poor Richard's
   b. Farley's
   c. The Office
   d. Meredith's Pub

37. What was the name of the street that the building in the opening credits is on?
   a. Mifflin Avenue
   b. Dunder Drive
   c. Mifflin Drive
   d. Dunder Avenue

38. Danny Cordray was named after who?
   a. Greg Daniels' brother
   b. One of the show's producers, Randy Cordray
   c. One of the show's writers, Darrell Cordray
   d. Greg Daniel's cousin

39. Who was Ryan Howard named after?
   a. A writer's family member
   b. Greg Daniels' brother
   c. Greg Daniels' best friend
   d. A major league baseball player

40. Which actors went to the same high schools?
   a. John Krasinski and BJ Novak
   b. Brain Baumgartner and Ed Helms
   c. Both A and B
   d. None of the actors went to the same high schools

41. Which actor thought the show would fail, so he kept his side jobs as a babysitter and a server?
   a. Jenna Fischer
   b. Phyllis Smith
   c. Angela Kinsey
   d. Oscar Nunez

42. True or False: The highlighted section of a document shown during the opening credits was a section of the Los Angeles Municipal Code.

43. Steve Carell placed what type of flag on his desk to honor the first version of The Office?

44. True or False: The theme song for The Office plays during the end credits in every season.

45. True or False: Steve Carell and Phyllis Smith are the same age, just like in the show.

46. Which actor auditioned for the role of Dwight?
    a. John Cho
    b. Seth Rogan
    c. Adam Scott
    d. All of the Above

47. Darryl's character was initially supposed to play the role of what character?
    a. Roy
    b. Kevin
    c. Jim
    d. Andy

48. Who was initially supposed to play the role of Pam?
    a. Erica Vittina Phillips ("Justine"-Darryl's ex-wife)
    b. Angela Kinsey
    c. It was always supposed to be Jenna Fischer
    d. Nancy Carell ("Carol"-Steve Carell's Wife)

49. Rainn Wilson accidently kicked sand into whose face during the filing of the episode, "Beach Games", which resulted in an injury to their cornea?
    a. John Krasinski
    b. Steve Carell
    c. Ed Helms
    d. Leslie David Baker

50. Which character from the Stamford branch was originally supposed to be a short-term character, but ended up being a regular character on the show?

51. Michael Scott had a fishbowl in his office. He originally had a goldfish, but he ends up having what type of fish?
    a. A guppy
    b. Another goldfish
    c. Siamese Fighting Fish
    d. Black Beta Fish

52. Why didn't Steve Carell watch the British version of The Office before acting in the American version?

53. Rainn Wilson wanted which actor to be his ex-girlfriend on the show?
   a. Katee Sackoff
   b. Amy Adams
   c. Lucy Lawless
   d. Tricia Helfer

54. Charles Miner's previous employer's name was actually a reference to the street where the show was being filmed. What was the name of that street?
   a. Miner Street
   b. Saticoy Street
   c. Sunset Street
   d. Mifflin Street

55. True or False: The network executive didn't know that Steve Carell was going to be in the finale episode.

ANSWERS

SEASON ONE

1. Grasshopper
2. A. Library
3. The wastepaper basket
4. B. '78 280Z
5. C. $1200
6. C. $3,000
7. A. A childhood trauma or out of a disaster
8. Daffy Duck
9. The Gold Plan
10. B. Therapeutic Massage
11. True
12. The Lion
13. C. $1,200
14. C. Scranton Travel Inc.
15. A. 150 Adams Avenue, Scranton, PA 18503
16. A. Atlantic City
17. B. Ebola and Mad Cow Disease
18. C. Spontaneous Dento-Hydroplosion
19. 300 Feet
20. B. Very slowly
21. D. Industrial Coal Elevator
22. "Teamwork"
23. Ice cream sandwiches
24. Yellow
25. False. During their engagement, Roy and Pam planned their wedding to be in September, but ended up cancelling
26. True
27. A. 17%
28. C. He cut expenses
29. A. A young Guatemalan guy who used to work at the office
30. Michael's "World's Best Boss" mug in Jell-o.
31. Honesty, Empathy, Respect, Open-mindedness
32. Jewish
33. False. Oscar receives the Eskimo card
34. "You're Hired" "and you can work here as long as you want"
35. Next to his desk
36. D. "What's the scuttlebutt"?

37. A. Operation "Morale Improvement"
38. "Absolutely I do."
39. True
40. C. Black
41. D. "Meredith, good news: you're not actually a year older, because you work here where time stands still."
42. C. "Meredith, Happy Birthday. You're the best. Love, Pam."
43. B. On Friday
44. Ryan
45. A. Red
46. B. A newspaper
47. A. Lunch time
48. "Blessed be those who "sit and wait"."
49. True
50. Jazz
51. B. Eating before a game
52. Farley's
53. Naked Aggression
54. The New Pam 6.0
55. A. Decisiveness
56. B. Small Businessman, USA Today, American Way
57. Starbucks
58. B. The employees did cocaine
59. A. Blue Blast and Artic Chill
60. He tells Ryan to put the Blue Blast in the trunk and the Artic Chill in the passenger's cup holder
61. C. A rubber band ball
62. B. Rite Aid "Night Swept"
63. B. Drakkar Noir
64. D. Filet-o-fish wrappers
65. Because Roy has a truck
66. C. A very symmetrical face
67. Toyota Corolla
68. Green Ford Ranger
69. A. His employees
70. True
71. D. Black, "World Anime Expo, Philadelphia 2002"
72. False. He told Dwight to pick the new healthcare plan
73. He says he would "be all over" Katy if he wasn't dating Pam
74. C. Moms
75. Michael Scott
76. "Little Drummer Boy"
77. "Hilary Rodham Clinton"
78. He was making fun of her ethnicity

79. He brings his own water to work
80. B. Green
81. Dairy
82. Ice Cream Cake
83. "Happy Bird-Day"
84. A charity for Cerebral Palsy
85. $25 per mile

SEASON TWO

1. B. Hidden, because he doesn't want to look at them and get cocky
2. A. At home in a display case above his bed
3. C. "Show me the money" award
4. Once every billion years
5. A. The "05/05/05" Party, a luau and the tsunami relief fundraiser
6. B. Because of Jan
7. C. Meredith
8. "Having a bathroom is a privilege."
9. B. Creed
10. A. Toby
11. C. Meredith and Creed
12. A. Glass of Red Wine
13. Teri
14. The "Don't go in there after me" award
15. His girlfriend (Stacy)
16. C. Randall
17. A. A blow-up doll
18. D. Classical and oldies
19. B. Paper football scoreboard
20. C. Oscar and Kevin's paper football game
21. D. Because Angela hates it
22. Toby
23. C. 126
24. A. Blue and white
25. A. Bill
26. B. Local stores and restaurants
27. Cookies
28. C. The eternal burning of competition
29. Gold, silver, blue (blue represents bronze)
30. Flonkerton
31. 10 over 30, 30-year total
32. True
33. A. Box of Paper Snowshoe Racing
34. A. Kevin and Phyllis
35. Phyllis
36. Blue – (Bronze)
37. D. 5:00 PM

38. Gold
39. For closing on his condo
40. A. Silver
41. Blue- (Bronze)
42. A water cooler jug
43. Desert Island, Who Would you Do, Would you Rather
44. False: The Bible, A Purpose Driven Life and the DaVinci Code so she can burn it
45. The DaVinci Code
46. True
47. A. waterproof matches, iodine tablets, beet seeds, protein bars and NASA blanket inside of the book
48. B. Legends of the Fall, My Big Fat Greek Wedding, Legally Blonde, Bridges of Madison County and Ghost
49. Blue
50. Fargo, Edward Scissorhands, Dazed and Confused, Breakfast Club, The Princess Bride
51. The Crow
52. Cumberland Mills
53. C. Monster.com, Google and Craigslist
54. A. Goju-Ryu Karate
55. Lackawanna County
56. Awesome Blossom
57. Pam
58. $25.00
59. D. Tom
60. W.B. Jones Heating & Air
61. B. Suite 210
62. He thinks he is a terrorist
63. Email surveillance
64. D. Penguin
65. B. Guitar
66. "Islands in the Stream", by the Bee Gees
67. A. Ryan
68. C. A shower radio
69. Lake Wallenpaupack
70. The Navy
71. False
72. Lake Wallenpaupack Princess
73. June 10th
74. Country Crock
75. C. Billy Merchant
76. D. Four extra strength Aspirin
77. Kurt

78. Hooters
79. Roy and Pam's celebrity name
80. A. New York
81. February 13th
82. C. Pizza from Cojino's Pizza
83. B. Around 66 degrees
84. Australia
85. B. June 8th
86. A. Stanley, Meredith, Kevin and Toby
87. Sasha
88. Jake
89. Fundle Bundle
90. C. Phil
91. A poster of kids dressed up
92. Mind control (telekinetic powers)
93. A soup kitchen
94. "Afghanistanis" with AIDS
95. B. At Chili's
96. Las Vegas
97. Phyllis
98. Scrantonicity
99. On Casino Night
100. Her mom

SEASON THREE

1. Liz Clayborn
2. B. Gray
3. A. A kurta
4. Monkey Brains
5. Carol
6. B. She doesn't have a date
7. False
8. Pictures of him kissing Carol
9. A. The Union of the Monkey
10. A Cheerleader
11. C. Wali
12. A. Beyonce- "Crazy in Love"
13. 30 years
14. Stills
15. C. Jim's old job (Junior Sales Associate or Salesman)
16. Purple
17. Angela
18. B. Toby
19. "Gay-dar"
20. Sharper Image
21. C. Brookstone
22. A. The day after tomorrow
23. B. HP
24. DUI
25. A. They froze it
26. 2
27. C. "Hope this helps."
28. A. A three month paid vacation and a company car
29. C. Europe
30. A Chinese baby
31. $1,000
32. Angela
33. A. Northeastern Mid-Market Office Supply Convention
34. D. A train
35. A. Their brothers
36. True
37. D. 3
38. B. White

39. C. Michael Scott
40. C. Room 308
41. A. Room 556
42. B. Hammermill Products
43. A. Allen
44. A. He thinks about stuff that he sees or he dreams them.
45. Movie Monday
46. C. Exit 40
47. That the vacuum could become the new manager
48. B. The women
49. D. A corporate lease
50. A. Something German with decent gas mileage
51. A. Mike from the West Side Market, 6
52. An old oil drum
53. By flying into the glass doors
54. B. The warehouse workers
55. "too small"
56. She confused it with the movie "28 Days" and was watching for Sandra Bullock to show up in the movie.
57. B. There are no pictures on the video tape boxes.
58. 364 days
59. "Lazy Scranton"
60. Suite 200
61. C. 1987
62. Cor-not University
63. C. Stealing, robbing, kidnapping the president's son and holding him for ransom
64. "The Bell of The Ball"
65. Black
66. Cindy
67. True
68. False. Creed sings the song "Spinnin' N" by Creed Bratton (Himself)
69. Todd Packer
70. A. Dr. Perry
71. Harvey
72. "Long Tim" is referring to when Michael's talking computer said "me love you long tim"
73. True
74. B. 80 pounds
75. B. 2 resume packets, 1 trivia packet-Professional Resume, Athletic and Special Skills Resume and Dwight Schrute Trivia.
76. Dwight
77. Michael
78. "Gay-cation"

79. False: He was scraping gunk off his wall sockets with a metal FORK and gave himself a nasty shock.
80. Dwight
81. Jump start a car and how to take off a woman's bra.
82. C. Gordon
83. A. Elizabeth
84. D. M&M's
85. Altoid
86. He didn't get to walk Phyllis down the aisle. Phyllis' father got out of his wheelchair and walked her down the aisle.
87. C. Red
88. "Phlob"
89. "Easy Rider"
90. B. Uncle Al
91. C. Whatchamacallit, PayDay, 100 Grand, Snickers
92. B. Economics
93. Motel Art
94. A "Chunky"
95. Potato Salad
96. It was in his car all day in the sun
97. That she kissed Jim on the Casino night
98. C. He would rather sit at home than go out to the movies with her
99. Pepper sprays him in the face
100. D. 8 years
101. B. A historical house
102. 3 years
103. A. For not saving the excess oil from a Tuna can
104. C. A Repliee Q1 Expo female robot
105. C. Darryl
106. B. Pager
107. C. $11.00
108. True
109. During his apology video
110. A Demerit
111. B. A "Dissajulation"
112. False: He was reading LETT Magazine
113. American Girls Doll Store
114. The egg on the spoon challenge
115. Note taking
116. B. Pam
117. Dwight & Pam
118. Natural Breasts
119. C. Stanley
120. "Beardy"

121. Because "she's nuts"
122. "I hope you get the job"
123. "Don't forget us when you're famous"
124. She's "Kind of a Bitch"
125. B. The Terminator

SEASON FOUR

1.   Soymilk
2.   A celebrity sex tape
3.   B. Sprinkles
4.   A. Balloons
5.   He asks Meredith what type of pain killers she is taking
6.   B. Michael Scott DWSMPMC Rabies Awareness Pro-Am Fun Run Race
7.   They bleed
8.   C. Elizabeth the stripper
9.   A. $340
10. Fettuccine Alfredo
11. D. A lamp
12. Blackberry
13. B. The foreign exchange student who lived with him and his family.
14. B. Robert
15. Jim
16. "Lunch Party"
17. Pizza by Alfredo
18. Alfredo's Pizza Café
19. C. He is the kid steals hemp from his hemp farm
20. A. $63.50
21. Half off
22. B. 8 pizzas
23. Two swans
24. False: He stole it
25. C. Dwight and Andy
26. B. Dwight
27. Here Comes Treble
28. A. The Devil Wears Prada
29. Works for a telemarketing company
30. C. Trip Advisor
31. Table making demonstration
32. A bag of oats
33. Scrantonicity 2
34. A. Nick Figaro
35. D. America, Irrigation and Nighttime
36. The train yard across the street from the office building
37. The "Kit Kat" song
38. A. Second Life

39.   His character can fly
40.   A. Creed, Darryl, Andy, Kelly and Kevin
41.   A. Sue Grafton
42.   "D"
43.   At Poor Richard's Pub
44.   Stanley
45.   True
46.   "Middle-aged Black Man with sass. Big butt, Bigger heart."
47.   Oscar, Pam and Toby
48.   C. Madge
49.   Soda can
50.   A commercial copier
51.   Michael
52.   B. Toby
53.   D. Peach Pie (Nice Cobbler)
54.   Mushrooms
55.   A. "Fudgy the Whale"
56.   "Jan has plastic boobs!"
57.   Have one birthday party for everyone
58.   A post-it note
59.   B. 4 million dollars
60.   Hunter
61.   To bring it to her deposition
62.   Ryan
63.   B. Chinese food
64.   Andy, Angela, Pam and Jim
65.   Dwight
66.   A. Wine
67.   "Serenity by Jan"
68.   Sliding glass door
69.   The bench in the bedroom
70.   B. $200
71.   Hunter's album
72.   B. His apartment flooded
73.   Michael ran through the sliding glass door because he thought he heard the ice cream truck
74.   B. $10,000
75.   His old babysitter
76.   "St. Pauli Girl. Imported German Beer."
77.   Michael's Dundie
78.   Hunter's Music Album
79.   B. The Chair Model Lady
80.   D. Page 85
81.   "Sandy" (Her fat friend)

82. Her Landlady
83. "Wendy" (Wendy's Restaurant)
84. Frosty and a baked potato
85. B. Deborah Shoshlefski
86. B. Car accident
87. A. (The five families of the Scranton Business Park): Dunder Mifflin, Vance Refrigeration, DisasterKits Limited, W.B Jones Heating and Air and Cress Tool and Die.
88. C. The show never reveals her name.
89. Toby
90. Troy
91. Hank
92. "Did I stutter?"
93. His faceprint
94. Fluffy Fingers
95. True
96. C. Valley View High School
97. C. Practicing for a golf game
98. Fireworks
99. Holly Flax
100. Jan

SEASON FIVE

1. Three extra vacation days
2. B. 2,210 pounds
3. Pratt School of Design
4. Kelly
5. Phyllis
6. Michael Klump
7. C. 1:00 PM
8. A soda
9. C. 7 pounds
10. In exchange for discounts on Dunder Mifflin supplies and Outback Steakhouse gift certificates.
11. A watermelon
12. B. Bruce Myers
13. "When the baby emerges, Mark it secretly in a kind of a mark that only you can recognize, and no baby snatcher could ever copy."
14. Orbit
15. C. $1,200
16. B. $1,200
17. Holly
18. She starts working part time at the Dunder Mifflin Corporate office.
19. D. His Laptop
20. His surge protector
21. C. Crime Reduces Innocence Makes Everyone Angry I Declare
22. To do taxes
23. A squeaky gavel
24. To go out for a beer "right now" with Darryl
25. B. $5
26. A. Raggedy Ann
27. C. A Cheerleader
28. C. Alex
29. B. $100
30. Canada
31. A. Flash, Acrobat and Quark
32. C. Matsuki
33. B. A brownie
34. On Linden Ave, by the quarry
35. C. Creed
36. He's going to Thailand with some friend from high school

37. C. $4,300
38. A. $645
39. A new copier
40. C. Conrad
41. C. In less than 10 minutes
42. My horn can pierce the sky
43. D. Equal parts scotch, absinthe, rum, gin, vermouth, triple sec and two packs of Splenda.
44. False: Sunrise Rehabilitation
45. C. Awareness, education, control, acceptance and punching
46. False: $200 and he can owe him the rest
47. B. 31 MPH
48. Oscar's desk
49. D. 40
50. After coming back from Vietnam
51. A. 80
52. C. Kevin, Oscar, Meredith, Phyllis, Toby
53. Pam
54. B. Phyllis
55. The vending machines
56. A. $3500
57. Always Be Closing
58. C. Rose
59. B. A case of do-si-dos
60. Phyllis
61. A. Angela
62. A. Anybody from the warehouse
63. "Gross"
64. C. Sam
65. B. The Travel Inn
66. A. Everyone
67. Ice Cream Cake
68. Princess Lady
69. B. $7,000
70. She sold the engagement ring that Andy gave her
71. A.J.
72. A. Valentine's day
73. Phyllis and Stanley
74. Creed
75. B. Blue Cross
76. C. 5 golden tickets
77. His 15th year anniversary party
78. "C" shaped
79. "You have no idea how high I can fly."

80. A. Kevin
81. C. 134
82. Soccer
83. C. The Orange Team
84. C. Caution: Hot Water. Do Not Touch
85. Kelly
86. C. Haddie
87. Pam
88. C. Russell
89. A. $12,000
90. Pam and Phyllis
91. C. Take out his battery
92. Ohio
93. C. Jessica
94. Kelly and Andy
95. A. His best friend, Rolph.
96. Holly
97. At a tour of Dartmouth College
98. With a gun
99. Buffalo
100. When she hurts herself in volleyball then goes to get an x-ray of her foot.

SEASON SIX

1. Refrigerator box
2. B. Dwight, Michael and Andy
3. A. Eric and Megan
4. Cynthia (Stanley's Mistress)
5. Oscar
6. C. Dwight and Toby
7. Darryl's sister
8. Michael
9. D. Firm Cheddar, Cheddar style spread, Parmesan and Blue Cheese dressing
10. C. A Birdhouse
11. The want cash as their wedding gifts
12. A. "To love's eternal glory"
13. Hard boiled eggs
14. Cynthia
15. Niagara Falls
16. B. Jocelyn Webster
17. C. Romeo-Tango-G77746
18. B. 2
19. B. Nine and three-quarters
20. C. "Burger-on-the go"
21. He tore his scrotum
22. He did the splits and landed on his keys
23. B. Apricot
24. When someone poops on the upper part of the toilet
25. B. Grotti
26. A. Puerto Rico
27. A Mechanic
28. C. Pat
29. Frank and Beans
30. Blind Guy McSqueezy
31. C. Coco Leche
32. A koi fish
33. D. Pumpernickel
34. A scrapbook
35. Because of her age
36. 58
37. Plastic tubes all over the office with hamsters inside of them

38. C. "Belles, Bourbon and Bullets"
39. Voodoo Mama JuJu
40. B. "Naughty Nellie Nutmeg"
41. A. "Caleb Crawdad"
42. "Recyclops"
43. B. The CEO of Dunder Mifflin
44. D. Ryan
45. He says, "Thank you. Thank you, a lot."
46. True
47. To pay their college tuition
48. C. "The Michael Gary Scott Reading Room"
49. Laptop Batteries
50. The 12 days of Christmas
51. A. Phyllis
52. A. Matt
53. Sabre
54. B. Eric Ward
55. Dwight
56. Michael
57. C. A printer, a fax machine and a scanner
58. His cellphone
59. A. Scranton Hot Dogs from Scranton
60. Erin and Andy
61. C. To go to the Olympics
62. Jo Bennett
63. Great Danes
64. B. The president and Judy Judge
65. Angela
66. False: "Ultra-Feast"
67. B. Michael
68. She's scared
69. A. Cecilia Marie Halbert
70. B. 7 lbs 2 oz
71. Kevin
72. Mold
73. C. Green M&M's
74. He made "Megadesk"
75. A lump of coal
76. A. Her foster brother named, Reed
77. C. Angela, Creed, Meredith
78. A. Riddles
79. The dumpyard
80. C. Erin
81. "Date Mike"

82. D. 25
83. A. 19
84. B. O negative
85. Oscar
86. A. Jim, Pam and Dwight
87. A. Has an office party for her
88. C. A barrel of beets
89. Donna
90. Kelly Kapoor
91. B. Print in All Colors
92. Donna
93. Jim and Pam
94. A. Pam
95. False: Darryl and Andy make the video
96. The gym
97. Michael
98. A. Radon
99. Ant traps
100. C. Andy

SEASON SEVEN

1.   D. Luke
2.   The Nard Man
3.   Bagel Chips
4.   His nephew, Luke
5.   Insane Clown Posse
6.   False: The "Steamtown" Mall
7.   He had beet juice on his hands
8.   A. Toby
9.   B. Law and Order
10. C. Wine
11. True
12. They have a contract to procreate together
13. B. Erin
14. A baseball bat
15. B. An Ingrown hair
16. A. Donna
17. C. Danny Cordray
18. C. Osprey Paper
19. Kevin
20. B. Lance Armstrong
21. C. Michael Moore
22. True
23. C. $15,000 in savings
24. B. Oscar
25. To build anti-bodies
26. C. His business cards
27. She gets poop all over it
28. C. "Sconsey Cider"
29. Glee
30. True
31. C. French Ads
32. A. He changed the channel to check the scores of a sports game
33. "Hay Place"
34. B. Big Boobz
35. They want the domain "WUPHF" (Washington University Public Health Fund)
36. D. A candy apple
37. C. "Dwight's Caffeine Corner"

38. A. "Bring That Booty"
39. China
40. B. Motion Sensor lights
41. "Actually"
42. D. Coffee
43. Pigeons
44. Office Administrator
45. Party Planning Committee
46. C. Hello Kitty Laptop Sleeve
47. Snowball fight
48. False: He is a State Senator
49. C. In the conference room
50. He's jealous of her boyfriend, AJ, who gave her the toy
51. C. Jada
52. B. "Knights of the Night"
53. Temptation
54. True
55. Dave Matthews Band
56. B. Do a cartwheel
57. A. Mikanos
58. A gas station
59. B. "Ask Pam Beasley"
60. C. Chinese
61. B. Gabe
62. False: Hank
63. False: It is a cookie heart
64. Michael Scarn
65. B. 8 years
66. A mop
67. C. Oscar
68. Jan
69. C. "The hostages are under the stadium."
70. C. A piano
71. D. When Toby gets shot in the head by Goldenface
72. B. A puck
73. Helene
74. A. Billy
75. "Ever banged an entire bachelorette party, baby?"
76. C. G-9
77. D. Meredith, Angela, Phyllis and Karen
78. Todd Packer
79. B. "Somehow I Manage"
80. C. "Here I Go Again, Dot, Dot, Dot"
81. C. 10

82. D. "All Stars"
83. A puck
84. A. Michael Scarn, (voice of Stanley)
85. False: They trick him into going to Tallahassee
86. A. Half used candle
87. Pesto Sauce and Salsa
88. C. Ryan's Pesto Sauce
89. D. A flashlight
90. A. "Professor Copperfield's Miracle Legumes"
91. Dallas
92. B. In pots outside the office building near the warehouse
93. C. Kahlua Sombrero
94. C. 19 years
95. Boulder, Colorado
96. B. Ashton Kutcher
97. A. 9,986,000 minutes
98. B. Bull testicles
99. His toy semi-truck
100. Mittens
101. His Clients
102. A scarecrow doll
103. C. Rory Flenderson
104. Paintball
105. C. 4:00 PM
106. B. A basketball hoop
107. D. One week
108. True
109. C. "Great Bratton"
110. BOBODY
111. C. Branch Manager
112. A. Jacques Souvenier
113. B. A homeless person
114. Robert California
115. The Finger Lakes

SEASON EIGHT

1. D: 6
2. A: Andy
3. Jim, Dwight, Oscar, Darryl, Andy, Toby, Phyllis, Angela, Kevin
4. False
5. C. The Pyramid
6. Margarita Pizza
7. C: Andy will get a tattoo on his butt
8. C: 1995
9. $950,000
10. Tacos
11. B. Dwight
12. C. Soy
13. Dwight and Andy
14. True
15. True
16. "The Ultimate Guide to Throwing a Garden Party"
17. B. James Trickington
18. A. $2.00
19. Her cat, Phillip
20. C. The valet
21. A basil plant
22. C. Wendy
23. Bert
24. Gabe, Kelly and Toby
25. True
26. Osama Bin Laden
27. "Closing Time" by Semisonic
28. D. Dwight
29. C. Val
30. True
31. Harmonica
32. D. 9
33. "DM does GB"
34. False. It was an underground hide out for "the sensitive and fabulous". The farmhouse was turned into a refuge for pacifists.
35. "Papyr"
36. Dunder Mifflin flag
37. B. A women's name

38. Susan California
39. False
40. D. Dwight Schrute's Gym for Muscles
41. Phone books
42. "I want Christmas. Give me plain baby Jesus lying in a manger Christmas!"
43. An acre of property on the "light side" of the moon
44. C. Ruth
45. A. At the Office Christmas Party
46. The Black-Eyed Peas
47. D. Assistant Cross Country Coach at Bryn Mawr
48. Because the upstairs people (office workers) have sticks up their butts
49. $200 bouquet of flowers to Pam from Jim
50. False. Its name is Henrietta
51. A. 14 minutes
52. "Oh yeah!"
53. B. Triviocalypse
54. $1,000
55. Toilet
56. The Einsteins
57. True
58. C. 1200
59. C. 1995 Chateau Margaux
60. A. "Footloose" by Kenny Loggins
61. False. He lied about being on a jury
62. Ernesto's
63. B. Empanadas
64. Dwight
65. A. Nate
66. C. Creed
67. C. 9 pounds, 7 ounces
68. Circumcision
69. True
70. Valentine's Day
71. "Perfectenschlag"
72. Jim, Erin, Ryan, Stanley and Kathy
73. B. 243
74. "It was Dwight" and "Luwanda at the alcohol club"
75. C. Heather
76. Nellie Bertram
77. A. Dwell
78. False. He had appendicitis and can't think straight, so he got all the pillars wrong.

79. A. Convenience, Service, Building Loyalty
80. C. Gerald
81. Waffles
82. Brandon
83. C. 200 years old
84. True
85. Tabitha
86. B. Basildon
87. "The Black One"
88. Strike, Scream, Run
89. Tiffy
90. Yellow or green
91. C. Eggplant Parmesan
92. Jessica's friend, Lauren
93. Smokey Robinson
94. B. The Scranton Animal Welfare Society
95. Over $34,000
96. "Big Red Paper Company"
97. The Scranton salesman that Dwight and Jim made up
98. A diaper
99. D. Bob Kazamakis
100. Coconut Penis

SEASON NINE

1. C. Beet run-off
2. False. Angela tells Dwight he is the father
3. Miami, Ohio
4. Pediatrics Professor
5. Pam
6. D. Clean annex
7. 8:00 AM
8. A. "Operation: Give Back"
9. American Diabetes Association
10. Global Relief Foundation
11. A. Laura
12. Steve
13. Dothraki
14. False: Nellie made it up.
15. C. Jerry
16. B. EMF Hotspots
17. For her adoption paperwork
18. A. "Laverne's Pies, Tires Fixed Also"
19. "You stupid, dumb, doo-doo face."
20. A pumpkin (A jack-o-lantern)
21. George Michael
22. "Karma Chameleon", by Culture Club
23. "Faith", by George Michael
24. C. $10,000
25. D. Dumatril
26. Sexy Toby
27. Broccoli Rob
28. He had sex with a snowman
29. B. Kevin
30. Iris Black
31. "Bizwhiz"
32. C. 43-Foot Tartan Sloop
33. Iris Black
34. Argentina
35. His brother, Walter JR.
36. B. The Bahamas
37. A. Desalinating Device
38. The White Pages

39. Dwight
40. Prostate cancer charity
41. False. Her name is Molly
42. A. 415-YCL
43. "Queen of the Primer"
44. Stanley and Phyllis
45. Break his knees (A knee-capping)
46. A. Heymont Brake and Tire
47. B. Dwight and Angela
48. False. Angela tells Toby her pastor said that gayness "comes from breast feeding."
49. C. Dwight and Angela
50. D. "Grandma is a Great Cook"
51. Dwight
52. Belsnickel
53. D. All of the Above
54. A. Stuffed pig stomach
55. A. Zwarte Peit
56. Admirable
57. Darryl
58. Dwight and Jim
59. Jim
60. True
61. Pam
62. B. "Freak, "Four Eyes", "Sci-Fi Nerd", "Girl Puncher"
63. C. Nellie, Kevin, Darryl, Phyllis, Dwight
64. A swarm of bees
65. False. The first time Erin drank espresso was Season 5 Episode 27. She contradicts herself in Season 9 Episode 11 when she says that it is the first time she's ever tried espresso.
66. False. Oscar finds out there is hardwood flooring under the carpet when Dwight shot his gun inside the office, Oscar saw the hardwood flooring through the bullet hole in the floor: Season 7 Episode 24.
67. Pam
68. She was hired for the mural project
69. A. Dwight
70. Bridgeport Capital
71. Brian
72. Brian
73. True
74. B. X-men School
75. Bear-yl
76. Frank
77. C. Malaysian

78. Pam and Dwight
79. He protected Pam against Frank
80. B. "Chunky Lemon Milk"
81. A. "A Pretty Girl"
82. The White Pages
83. David hears Erin say, "you were gone for three months", to Andy while he was on the phone with Andy.
84. He hoses her off outside
85. Oscar
86. C. Red Ford Mustang
87. "Nibbles"
88. Pam
89. A. Henry
90. The beaks of a crow
91. "50 Shades of Grey"
92. Dwight
93. Andy
94. A. "Skrald Mand" ("Dumpster Man")
95. C. Angela
96. A 5 Hour Energy drink
97. Iced tea, three sugars and five creams
98. B. "HRPDC Chemical Handling Protocols"
99. At the office
100. A. Lorelei
101. From a jewelry store
102. Assistant to the Assistant to the Regional Manager
103. "America's Next A Capella Sensation"
104. B. Cincinnati, Ohio
105. C. Ezra Cornell
106. State Senator
107. The Grass Roots
108. B. Creed
109. Best man
110. "A Keleven"
111. Rachel
112. True
113. PhD in School Psychology
114. So they could get severance packages
115. Andy
116. Orange Dodge Challenger
117. A. PBS
118. A. A DVD
119. He gives him a cake that says, "Get out".
120. True

121. C. 12 years
122. C. Poland
123. New York
124. False. He never changed it.
125. "There's a lot of beauty in <u>ordinary</u> <u>things</u>. Isn't that the point?"

BONUS ANSWERS

1. True
2. True
3. True
4. B.J. Novak
5. Phyllis Smith
6. False: She originally auditioned for the role of Pam.
7. Amy Poehler (Leslie Knope)
8. True
9. A. Farley's
10. D. All of the above
11. False: Froggy 101 is an actual radio station in Scranton.
12. A. John Krasinski
13. C. Greg Daniels
14. True
15. Staples
16. Season 3
17. True
18. B. Costa Rica
19. The Office creator and executive producer
20. C. Angela, Creed, Oscar and Phyllis
21. C. Angela
22. B. Greg Daniels
23. False: It was a replica of a rest stop that the crew built
24. D. All of the Above
25. False: During the 1st season of The Office, the show was almost cancelled.
26. A. Scranton Chamber of Commerce
27. A. FX or HBO
28. A. David Denman
29. C. He thought the names of the cities were funny
30. 2005
31. B. A reality show about Amish people
32. C. The Farm
33. True
34. True
35. Season 4
36. C. The Office
37. A. Mifflin Avenue
38. B. One of the show's producers, Randy Cordray
39. D. A major league baseball player

40.   C. Both A and B: John Krasinski and BJ Novak went to Newton South High School together and Brain Baumgartner and Ed Helms both went to The Westminster Schools in Georgia.

41.   D. Oscar Nunez

42.   True

43.   A British Flag

44.   False: The theme song plays during the end credits after Season 4 starts and all the other season do not have the theme song playing during the end credits.

45.   False: Phyllis is 11 years older than Steve.

46.   D. All of the Above

47.   A. Roy

48.   A. Erica Vittina Phillips ("Justine"- Darryl's ex-wife)

49.   D. Leslie David Baker

50.   Andy (Ed Helms)

51.   D. Black Beta Fish

52.   He didn't want Ricky Gervais' character to influence the way he planned to portray Michael Scott's character.

53.   A. Katee Sackoff

54.   B. Saticoy Street

55.   True

Made in the USA
San Bernardino, CA
23 May 2020